"Are you a hard-driving, multitasking, conscientiously-striving professional? Then your ideas about success are probably all wrong—and you need *The Happiness Track*, Dr. Emma Seppälä's investigation into the counterintuitive factors that create career and life success. The best news of all? All these skills are well within your grasp."

—Daniel H. Pink, author of *Drive* and *A Whole New Mind*

"Emma Seppälä convinces us that reconfiguring our brain for happiness can change the way our lives unfold and the way we approach success. A worthwhile read for anyone who wants to achieve a successful and fulfilling life."

—Amy Cuddy, professor at Harvard Business School and author of *Presence*

"Backed by extensive research in psychology and neuroscience, *The Happiness Track* offers a wealth of insight for changing how we approach our work, our personal lives, and our relationships. It's a carefully researched, engaging look at how to improve ourselves without losing our authenticity or our sanity."

—Adam Grant, Wharton professor and *New York Times* bestselling author of *Give and Take*

"Through her research-backed strategies, Emma Seppälä not only teaches us how to thrive in our chosen profession but how to stay true to ourselves—and enjoy every moment of the process."

—Susan Cain, cofounder of Quiet Revolution and *New York Times* bestselling author of *Quiet*

"For decades, we've been tied to theories of success that have burned us out and driven us into the ground—because we don't know of any alternatives. *The Happiness Track* provides us with a highly-readable, science-backed solution to obtaining sustainable success, the sort of success we are all really striving for, that leaves us fulfilled, happy, and healthy."

—Scott Barry Kaufman, Ph.D., scientific director at the Imagination Institute at the University of Pennsylvania

"Emma Seppälä shows us how we can cultivate a meaningful and successful career and live happy, fulfilled lives by taking care of ourselves first. The world has needed Emma Seppälä's insight for a long time."

—Chade-Meng Tan, Google's "Jolly Good Fellow" and author of the *New York Times* bestseller *Search Inside Yourself*

"*The Happiness Track* offers us a magnificent overview of what the latest scientific research affirms are the most important ways we create both health and happiness in our lives. Emma Seppälä is on the cutting-edge of crucial new insights and practices that can help us redefine success as she illuminates the ways compassion toward oneself and others is the bedrock of living a life of connection and deep meaning. What a gift to be able to take in her words of wisdom and cultivate deeper ways we can all thrive!"

—Daniel J. Siegel, M.D., author of *Mindsight, Brainstorm,* and *The Mindful Therapist*; executive director of the Mindsight Institute; and clinical professor at the UCLA School of Medicine

"Dr. Seppälä turns cutting edge science into a fast-paced, practical book with profound implications. Remarkably, happiness feels good because it *is* good for our health, relationships, and work. Drawing on research from neuroscience and psychology, and her own groundbreaking work at Stanford, she gives us six powerful ways to turn greater well-being into greater success."

—Rick Hanson, Ph.D., author of *Hardwiring Happiness*

"This book is a breath of fresh air, helping to bust the myth that we need to do more, better, faster, and more efficiently to be happy. Seppälä shows us that by letting go of our relentless striving to achieve, we can realize the calm, joy, and compassion that are already here in the present moment."

—Kristin Neff, Ph.D., author of *Self-Compassion*

"Emma Seppälä smashes cultural definitions of 'success' with a wealth of research-grounded insight about unlocking creativity and a meaningful life. Seppälä is a fast-rising star, and I predict that her work will positively impact countless people for years to come."

—Peter Sims, author of *Little Bets* and cofounder & CEO of
The Silicon Guild

"For many, happiness remains elusive. Dr. Seppälä's book uses the latest scientific research to show us a path to real happiness. It's not what many of us think. Be ready to change your life for the better."

—James R. Doty, M.D., founder and director of the Center
for Compassion and Altruism Research and Education,
professor of neurosurgery at the Stanford University School
of Medicine, and author of *Into the Magic Shop*

THE HAPPINESS TRACK

HOW TO APPLY THE SCIENCE OF HAPPINESS
TO ACCELERATE YOUR SUCCESS

EMMA SEPPÄLÄ, Ph.D.

HarperOne
An Imprint of HarperCollinsPublishers

FIRST HARPERCOLLINS PAPERBACK EDITION PUBLISHED IN 2017

Designed by Level C

Library of Congress Cataloging-in-Publication Data
is available upon request.

ISBN 978-0-06-234401-4

17 18 19 20 21   LSC(H)   10 9 8 7 6 5 4 3 2 1

For my beloved
Pums & Dadda,
Andrew & Michael

CONTENTS

Introduction   1

1 **STOP CHASING THE FUTURE**
   Why Happiness and Success Are Found in the Present   15

2 **STEP OUT OF OVERDRIVE**
   Tap into Your Natural Resilience   39

3 **MANAGE YOUR ENERGY**
   The Hidden Benefits of Calm   67

4 **GET MORE DONE BY DOING MORE OF NOTHING**
   The Secret to Accessing Creativity   95

5 **ENJOY A SUCCESSFUL RELATIONSHIP . . .
   WITH YOURSELF**
   How You Relate to Yourself Affects Your Potential   121

6 **UNDERSTAND THE KINDNESS EDGE**
   Why Compassion Serves You Better Than Self-Interest   141

Acknowledgments   165

Notes   167

Index   203

About the Author   213

INTRODUCTION

Success is liking yourself, liking what you
do, and liking how you do it.
—*Maya Angelou*

One summer when I was in college, I interned for a major international newspaper in Paris, France. As the only intern there, I was very
busy. From 2 to 11 P.M., I ran between the second floor and the basement delivering messages and documents. I interacted with nearly
everyone, from the top editors to the printing staff. The second floor
housed a handful of executives in their windowed offices and a large
number of American writers and editors who sat bent over computers
in cubicles. In the basement were the blue-collar French press workers
who printed the newspapers.

The difference in atmosphere between the second floor and the
basement was striking. On the second floor, you could feel the tension in the air. The floor was quiet except for the sounds of typing
and printing. The editors—most of them overweight with dark circles
under their eyes—were huddled over their screens, keeping to themselves and eating pizza at their desks. But in the basement, the mood
was downright festive. French wine, cheese, and bread were all laid
out on a huge table. The printing staff laughed and joked; the atmosphere was vibrant. Whereas on the second floor no one talked to me
unless they needed something, I was always loudly welcomed when I

went into the printing room. Soon, I found myself wishing for more reasons to join that joyful atmosphere.

Working at the newspaper, going back and forth between these two groups got me thinking: Here was a team of people—editors, writers, and press workers—working through the night to finish and distribute a newspaper by dawn. Yes, it's true that the two groups performed different tasks and came from different cultures—but they were both working to meet the same urgent deadline. One mistake from either group and the paper missed its morning delivery. Night after night, despite the challenges, both groups successfully completed their jobs. Yet they went about it in opposite ways: one group was stressed, burned out, and unhealthy looking; the other happy, energetic, and thriving.

I believe most of us want to be like the French press workers: we want to do a good job—and we want to enjoy doing it. Everyone wants to be successful and happy. And yet achieving these two goals has never been more elusive.

Because of advances in technology, the pace of our lives is reaching overwhelming levels. Whether you're a CEO or a freelance art designer, you probably find yourself running from deadline to deadline, checking your mobile device for the latest e-mail or text, updating your social media status, and reading up on the latest blog or news; all while planning the dinner menu, navigating traffic, and anticipating an upcoming conference call. Projects need to be completed on shorter and shorter deadlines. With data and information readily available online, research needs to be in depth and rigorous. Customers need better service faster, not to mention cheaper. Your boss and colleagues expect immediate responses to their messages and requests.

To keep up with the demands of life, you probably sleep with your phone next to your bed and, more often than not, check e-mail first thing in the morning and right before going to bed. You also connect with your "friends" via social media platforms like Twitter, Facebook, or LinkedIn, responding to incoming notifications, to that must-watch video someone sent you, and to the implicit obligation to post updates and photos to stay in touch with the world. Meanwhile, e-mail and message in-boxes fill up no matter how long or hard you work to stay on top of them. Your weekdays are an endless race to complete the never-ending to-do list before you collapse into bed, exhausted, getting to sleep at a much later hour than your body would like.

Your weekends aren't much better. They are likely filled with domestic errands like laundry and grocery shopping, as well as work that has spilled over from the workweek. Vacations, few and far between, pack in stressful travel, visits with relatives, and maybe one or two days of extra sleep before you return to the grind. And even when you are on vacation, you find it hard to unplug from the world of work—so you check your devices to keep up with your job while sitting by the pool.

We have simply accepted overextension as a way of life.

We want to be good employees, so we work hard; we want to be good parents, so we try to spend more time with our kids; we want to be good spouses, so we cook meals, go to the gym, plan a date night; we want to be good friends, so we attend social activities—and we do all of this even though we're exhausted.

When the speed of our lives makes us feel stressed, drained, and overextended, we blame ourselves. After all, everyone else seems to be keeping up. To succeed, we believe we just need to hang in there and keep going—pushing past the pain, past our limits, and past our well-being.

When we do achieve our goals by rushing, straining, and keeping up, we don't necessarily feel good; we might experience a sense of relief, but that relief comes with a high price tag: burnout, disconnection, stress. But isn't the point of all that hard work and suffering to be happy? Isn't the idea that success will bring happiness?

THE MYTHS OF SUCCESS

Over the last decade, I have spent time with highly successful people. I studied alongside them at Yale, Columbia, and Stanford. I worked with them in Paris, New York City, Shanghai, and Silicon Valley. While I have been inspired by my colleagues as they launch nonprofits, get voted into Congress, write bestselling novels, become successful Broadway actors, found innovative start-ups, play major roles in humanitarian efforts across the world, and attain billionaire status as Wall Street bankers, I have also been saddened to see so many of these outwardly "successful" people drive themselves into the ground and end up chronically stressed and unhealthy. These people are highly talented with huge potential, yet sadly, in the process of reaching their goals, many of them burn out their greatest asset: themselves. They often drive their employees into the ground as well, creating a culture of stress all around them.

While on the one hand I was observing this phenomenon among my friends and former classmates, I was, on the other, studying and researching the psychology of health and happiness as a doctoral student at Stanford University. The deeper I delved into that literature, the more I was stunned to discover that the way we are taught to seek success—and what is culturally supported and encouraged—is plain wrong. Study upon study confirmed that what my friends and colleagues were doing—and what *I* was doing—in our search for success and happiness was actually backfiring.

Since then, I've come to appreciate that we are compromising our ability to be truly successful and happy because we are falling for common but outdated theories about success. We believe in these theories of success precisely because we see them play out routinely in the lives of successful people like my colleagues. From a young age we are taught that getting ahead means doing everything that's thrown at us (and then some) with razor-sharp focus and iron discipline—and at the expense of our happiness.

Here are the six major false theories that drive our current notions of success:

- **Never stop accomplishing.** Stay continuously focused on getting things done. To achieve more and stay competitive, you've got to move quickly from one to-do to another, always keeping an eye on what's next.

- **You can't have success without stress.** Stress is inevitable if you want success. Living in overdrive is the inescapable by-product of a fast-paced life. Suffering is inevitable and even necessary.

- **Persevere at all costs.** Work to exhaustion; spend every drop of mental energy you have staying on task despite distractions and temptations.

- **Focus on your niche.** Immerse yourself in your area of knowledge; by focusing exclusively on your field and becoming an expert in it, you'll know how to best solve its problems.

- **Play to your strengths.** Align your work with your talents. Do what you do best, and stay away from your weak areas. To discover your talents and weaknesses, be your own toughest critic.

- **Look out for number one.** Look out primarily for yourself and your interests so you can successfully outperform the competition.

These theories of success permeate our culture. They are ingrained in us from the time we attend elementary school ("Don't daydream!" "Focus!" "Work harder!"). But while these theories are widely popular and appear to make a lot of sense, they are, in fact, incredibly flawed. While some people have attained success this way, they have done so at great cost. In fact, research demonstrates that these theories actually hurt your potential for success and happiness because they lead to a host of negative consequences: they harm your ability to connect productively with others, impede work creativity, diminish your energy, prevent you from performing at your best, and make you less resilient in the face of challenge and failure. Research suggests that you are also more likely to end up burned out, isolated, and suffering from poor physical and mental health.

The way we go about finding success—fueled by a cultural message to "do it all," supported by technology that keeps us plugged in 24/7, and driven by these myths of success—is simply unsustainable. Everyone feels the crushing pressure of this approach to success—the great myth overarching all the other myths of success is that we have to sacrifice happiness in the short term to be successful and fulfilled in the long term. However, this approach not only keeps us from being as productive as we can be but actually makes us deeply *un*happy. In the last year, have you felt

- overextended with no solution or end in sight?

- trapped in a never-ending rat race of to-do's to accomplish?

- out of time to do the things you want to do?

- unable to spend time with your loved ones?

- feeling guilty for doing things you enjoy rather than being productive?

- failing to find meaning or fulfillment in your day-to-day?

You're not alone. Stress levels in the United States are increasing at an alarming rate, according to a study[1] by the Regus Group, which found 58 percent of Americans claiming that their stress is rising. Anxiety is the leading cause for mental health treatment in the United States, costing the nation over $42 billion per year.[2] The use of antidepressants among Americans of all ages has risen by 400 percent in the last decade.[3]

According to a 2014 Gallup study,[4] a parallel crisis is going on in workplaces nationwide: 50 percent of employees are unengaged (present but uninspired), while 20 percent are actively disengaged (that is, very unhappy at work), costing the US economy over $450 billion per year.

Decades of research have shown that happiness is not the *outcome* of success but rather its *precursor*. In other words, if you want to succeed, you have to be more like the French press workers in the basement.

WHAT'S HAPPINESS GOT TO DO WITH IT?

A few years ago, I gave a talk on the psychology of happiness to a group of accountants at a Fortune 100 firm in New York City. About forty people were crowded into the conference room. As I started my talk, I could tell that some of the audience members were keenly interested in the topic, while others sat at the back of the room and snickered. The latter were obviously required to be at the talk but didn't think this "soft" subject would be of value.

I didn't blame them. After all, we rarely hear about happiness as the secret to success. We are, in fact, taught the opposite.

The colleague who invited me to speak to the accounting firm had warned me that the science of happiness might not resonate with his data-focused colleagues. He advised me to start with facts and figures about the cost of negative emotions and the benefits of happiness.

Since I would be dealing with accountants, I should just let the numbers speak for themselves. Sure enough, by the time I finished going through the hard facts, the snickering had died down. By the end of the talk, even the cynics at the back of the room shared with me that they were convinced by what they called "an avalanche of persuasive data."[5]

Even if we don't frequently hear about the connection between happiness and success, we know intuitively the powerful impact our emotions have on us. After all, a nasty comment from a colleague or a morning fight with a spouse can disrupt our productivity and focus for the rest of the day. Our emotions and state of mind heavily influence everything we do. Think of how differently your interactions and productivity are when you feel stressed, sad, or angry versus when you are happy, relaxed, and grateful.

Happiness—defined as a state of heightened positive emotion—has a profound positive effect on our professional and personal lives. It increases our emotional and social intelligence, boosts our productivity, and heightens our influence over peers and colleagues. These are the very ingredients that allow us to be successful without having to sacrifice our health and psychological well-being.

Barbara Fredrickson from the University of North Carolina, along with other researchers who study the impact of positive emotions, have found that happiness brings out our best potential in four concrete ways.[5]

Intellectually. Positive emotions help you learn faster, think more creatively, and resolve challenging situations. For example, Mark Beeman at Northwestern University has shown that people have an easier time solving a puzzle after watching a short comedy clip. Fun, by easing tension and activating pleasure centers in the brain, helps spark neuronal connections that facilitate greater mental flexibility and creativity.[6] It's no surprise then that multiple studies have shown that happiness makes people 12 percent more productive.[7]

Psychologically. If you're like most people, you probably fall prey to the ebbs and flows of your state of mind. Your moods, not external factors, determine how your day will go. You can be on a beautiful beach yet feel miserable because you are upset at a family member. Or you can be blissful in bumper-to-bumper traffic because you just found out that you and your partner are expecting a child—positive emotions help keep you emotionally balanced regardless of circumstances. How? Research by Barbara Fredrickson[8] and others shows that positive emotions help you bounce back from stress much more quickly. By helping you rapidly recuperate from negative emotions, they effectively shorten the time you feel stressed, angry, or depressed and make you generally more optimistic.[9]

Let's say your job requires you to to interact with a client, colleague, or manager who is critical and harsh. As a consequence, you may find it challenging to keep giving your best day after day. However, if you are able to maintain a high level of positive emotion, you will recover more quickly after each interaction. Your optimism will provide a psychological and physiological buffer against the stress caused by that person. You can maintain your productivity and peace of mind more easily.

Socially. There's no doubt that relationships at work—be they with managers, colleagues, employees, or clients—are essential to success. Positive emotions strengthen existing relationships. For example, shared laughter—the expression of positive emotion—makes people more open and willing to cooperate.[10]

A number of studies show that happy employees make for a more congenial workplace. In particular, happy, friendly, and supportive co-workers tend to

- build higher-quality relationships with others at work[11]
- boost co-workers' productivity levels[12]
- increase co-workers' feeling of social connection[13]
- improve commitment to the workplace[14]

- increase levels of engagement with their job[15]
- provide superior customer service even if they don't stand to benefit[16]

Research shows that negative feelings like anxiety and depression, unlike positive emotions, make us more self-centered.[17] In contrast, positive emotions boost our inclination to connect with others in productive ways. Fredrickson shows[18] that happiness increases our sense of belonging, allowing us to see things from others' perspective and thereby more likely to make a positive difference in their lives. It dramatically increases our ability to build relationships and friendships. In turn, we feel more connected, more confident, and more supported by our growing networks. Our happiness also affects our colleagues' productivity. Just as difficult co-workers can create a challenging atmosphere, people who are positive and supportive create an uplifting atmosphere. By being happy, you make those around you happier. Research[19] by social scientists James Fowler of University of California, San Diego, and Nicolas Christakis of Harvard University suggests that happiness tends to spread up to three degrees of separation from you—to those close to you, your colleagues and acquaintances, and even strangers you will never know. This is how you create a culture of happiness in your workplace, home, or community.

Physically. Fredrickson has found that positive emotions improve physical well-being by increasing strength and cardiovascular health as well as by improving coordination, sleep, and immune function. Additionally, positive emotions are associated with reduced inflammation.[20] In other words, being happier helps to keep you healthier, even if you work in a high-intensity or stress-inducing environment. In fact, positive emotions speed up recovery from the cardiovascular impact of stress.[21] Preliminary studies have also shown that lightening up with laughter normalizes levels of the stress hormone cortisol, boosts immune function, and reduces inflammation.[22]

Knowing that happiness leads to success is not enough, however. That's why I wrote this book: to show you exactly how your happiness can maximize your resilience, creativity, productivity, charisma, and many other critical skills for success. You will learn skills like how to be productive without chronic stress, how to achieve more without burning out—in other words, how to maximize your professional potential *and* personal fulfillment.

THE SIX KEYS TO HAPPINESS AND SUCCESS

In the following chapters, I will share empirically validated data demonstrating that the path to long-term success and well-being is often the opposite of what we've been taught. We will examine how the counterproductive theories of success that dominate our culture backfire and undermine our best efforts. Drawing on the latest findings from psychology, organizational behavior, and neuroscience—research on resilience, creativity, mindfulness, compassion, and more—I will show you how the following six strategies for attaining happiness and fulfillment are actually the key to thriving professionally.

1. **Live (or work) in the moment.** Instead of always thinking about what's next on your to-do list, focus on the task or conversation at hand. You will become not only more productive but also more charismatic.

2. **Tap into your resilience.** Instead of living in overdrive, train your nervous system to bounce back from setbacks. You will naturally reduce stress and thrive in the face of difficulties and challenges.

3. Manage your energy. Instead of engaging in exhausting thoughts and emotions, learn to manage your stamina by remaining calm and centered. You'll be able to save precious mental energy for the tasks that need it most.

4. Do nothing. Instead of spending all your time focused intently on your field, make time for idleness, fun, and irrelevant interests. You will become more creative and innovative and will be more likely to come up with breakthrough ideas.

5. Be good to yourself. Instead of only playing to your strengths and being self-critical, be compassionate with yourself and understand that your brain is built to learn new things. You will improve your ability to excel in the face of challenge and learn from mistakes.

6. Show compassion to others. Instead of remaining focused on yourself, express compassion to and show interest in those around you and maintain supportive relationships with your co-workers, boss, and employees. You will dramatically increase the loyalty and commitment of your colleagues and employees, thereby improving productivity, performance, and influence.

These six strategies will greatly improve your psychological and physical well-being. They will help you be happier and live a life of meaning and purpose, and—as I show throughout the book—enhance success. The strategies are not complicated; applying them to your daily life does not require complex training or huge lifestyle changes. In fact, these strategies tap into resources you already have.

You already have the capacity to come up with brilliant ideas, to remain calm in the face of overwhelming demands, to stay present when your mind pulls you away, to be kind to yourself and others, to sit with your thoughts and rest when the world tells you to go, go, go. Each chapter will provide concrete how-to's to help you get there.

Whatever your personal endeavor—full-time dad in Chicago, Fortune 500 CEO in Dallas, community activist in Oakland, or ballerina in New York City—I hope this book will provide you with relief. Relief in the knowledge that you already have all it takes to be happy *and* successful; that a stress-free and fulfilled life is not only possible but also the secret to personal and professional success. You have the ability to tap into the festive productivity of the French printing team, and I'll show you how. The research is clear: happiness is the fast-track to success.

———

ONE

STOP CHASING THE FUTURE

WHY HAPPINESS AND SUCCESS
ARE FOUND IN THE PRESENT

No valid plans for the future can be made by
those who have no capacity for living now.
—*Alan Watts*[1]

When you travel to Silicon Valley—the land of Facebook, Twitter, Google, and Stanford University—you notice almost immediately that there is a buzz in the air. Whether it's in the downtown Palo Alto cafés where you inevitably overhear excited conversations between start-up entrepreneurs and would-be investors or on the Stanford campus where brilliant students sit in beautiful lecture halls listening to Nobel prize–winning professors—the buzz of excitement and achievement is practically tangible. The thrill of opportunity, invention, and success permeates the atmosphere.

But if you listen closely, you will hear another distinctive buzz alongside it: the buzz of chronic anxiety.

When I arrived at Stanford for graduate school, I was shocked by how many suicides there were during my first year there. Here we were on one of the most stunning and sunny campuses in the world, biking down palm-lined roads to get to class and surrounded by talented scholars and classmates, yet there was so much misery.

Saddened by these events, a fellow Stanford student and I were inspired to offer happiness and mindfulness workshops to students, and I helped cofound Stanford's first psychology of happiness course. In teaching these classes, I got to know Stanford undergraduate and graduate students from all fields. I began to understand where the anxiety and misery were coming from, not only at Stanford but also throughout Silicon Valley and, in fact, among all the overachiever communities I had known at Yale, Columbia, and in Manhattan.

Focused on the future and on everything they needed to do, students were permanently anxious. Everyone was frantically knocking out one achievement after another. Before they had finished one task, their minds were already on to the next thing they could accomplish in the name of productivity and success. As a consequence, they were unable to be present and celebrate their current accomplishments, not to mention enjoy their life.

Jackie[2] was one of the many stellar students I taught. She was no stranger to success. Already as a teenager, she received acclaim and media attention for her dedication to community service. At fourteen, she founded Everybody Dance Now, a nonprofit dedicated to teaching dance to underprivileged youths to help them stay off the streets and develop confidence. In addition to her commitment to community service, she excelled in high school, winning a number of grants and scholarships based on her academic achievements and becoming California's Junior Miss before landing a coveted undergraduate admission to Stanford. There, she continued to be celebrated in the public eye when she expanded her nonprofit nationally, was featured on MTV's America's Best Dance Crew, and was named one of *Glamour* magazine's Top Ten College Women.

Jackie knew she had to be successful to get into college. What

she didn't know, however, was that she would have to keep collect-
ing achievements after she got there. She was troubled to find that,
once at Stanford, everyone kept frantically focusing their efforts on
achieving more awards, further acclaim, and greater successes. "Even
when you introduced people, you would always mention their past
accomplishments as part of the introduction: this is so-and-so who
has achieved these impressive things," Jackie shared. She felt burned
out, but her professors told her that she would need to keep col-
lecting achievements and should do so quickly to keep up with her
classmates. "My friends were starting nonprofits that were receiving
national recognition, becoming Rhodes Scholars, being nominated
by *Forbes* as '20 under 20,' or were Olympic-level athletes. One of my
friends was the youngest city council member in California and the
third political candidate to be backed by Oprah—as a college senior!"

Jackie gives the example of applying for a scholarship at nineteen,
as a junior in college. As part of this scholarship, she was asked to
describe which graduate school program she planned to pursue, what
classes she would be taking there, the job she would get on her way
out, her ten-year career plan, the world problems she was planning
to solve in her career, and their policy implications—in addition to
describing the extensive leadership experience she was meant to have
demonstrated by that point in her life! "You are pushed into thinking
so far into your future. . . . You're basically on a hamster racetrack. A
rat race."

Carole Pertofsky,[3] director of Wellness and Health Promotion at
Stanford, with whom I founded Stanford's first psychology of happiness class, explained the "Stanford Duck Syndrome" to me. On the
surface, the students look like peaceful ducks, serenely gliding along
in the sun, contentedly basking in the splendor and grace of their success. However, if you look under the surface, there is a dark underside:
the ducks' legs are furiously pedaling as they struggle to stay afloat

and to keep moving. Carole recounts the story of a student who came up to her after the first class of the happiness course. The student announced that she had to drop out. "When I asked her why, she said that it went against everything she had been taught: 'My parents told me that my job in life was to be very, very successful. As I got older, I asked my parents what I needed to do to be very successful, and they said to work very, very hard. As time went by, I asked them, how do I know when I'm working hard enough, and they said, "When you're suffering."'" Carole explains that this mentality is the undercurrent of Stanford overachievers. There is a constant focus on achievement, and you are meant to pay the price by sacrificing your well-being.

This rat race does not just take place at Stanford or in Silicon Valley. It's *everywhere*. Whether you're a web designer, teacher, firefighter, or army officer, you are encouraged to keep checking things off the to-do list, amassing accomplishments, and focusing your efforts on the future. There's always something more you can do to further yourself at work: an extra project or responsibility you can take on, more schooling you can complete to ensure a promotion, or an additional investment to wager on just in case! There's always that coworker who is putting in longer hours, showing you that you too can and should do more. And so you strive nonstop to exceed your goals, constantly playing catch-up with your ambitious to-do list.

Why? Because you live by the faulty theory that, if you want to succeed, you need to continually be getting things done and moving on to the next goal as quickly as possible. Your mind is always on the next task, the next accomplishment, the next person you need to talk to. In the process, you sacrifice the present—forgoing personal happiness, enduring negative feelings and tremendous stress—because you believe the eventual payoff is worth it. As a consequence, you get caught up in frantic and anxious workaholism. You may find yourself asking, "What am I doing right now to help reach my future goals?"

If you're not asking yourself this question, t'
ner, or colleagues probably are. And if you
may feel bad. Thus the need to constantly be
improve yourself.

You're caught up in the compulsion to constantly ac.
adding meat to your bio and feathers to your cap. You haven't
one task before your mind is on to the next one. You work har
clear things off your to-do list, and then immediately fill it up again.
You might be working on a presentation or article, but your mind
is already on the topic you will cover in the next one. Even at home
you might be doing dishes, but your mind is making a mental list of
other chores you need to tackle.

This tendency to focus on getting things done is of course not categorically negative— accomplishments are good things! Yet constantly
focusing on the next thing ironically ends up keeping you from the very
success you are chasing. When everyone embraces the view that each
minute is an opportunity to accomplish more and move ahead, you get
caught up in this perspective and don't stop to question whether it's
working for you. And you may even pride yourself on your willpower.

Research[4] shows that children's ability to delay gratification—the
willpower to stop doing something that will bring them immediate
satisfaction so that they can receive an even bigger reward later—
predicts success in life. In a classic study, children were offered a treat
(like a marshmallow or cookie) and told that if they didn't eat it right
away, they would get double or more later. Those who were able to
wait ended up doing better in life as adults.

Sounds good in general, right? The problem comes, however, when,
as adults, we keep delaying our happiness in favor of getting more
things done so that we can be even happier later—or so we think.
This delaying process can go on forever, turning into workaholism,
which damages the very success and happiness we are seeking.

THE ANTICIPATORY JOY TRAP

In *Authentic Happiness*,[5] psychologist Martin Seligman tells the story of a pet lizard who refused to eat and was slowly starving to death. The owner was at a loss as to how to save his lizard's life. One day, as the owner was eating a sandwich, the lizard riled up its energy and pounced on it. The lizard wasn't dying from lack of food. He would just rather starve to death than live a life devoid of the opportunity to *hunt*.

The hunt captures us too. It is the reason we get so caught up in chasing achievements. This joy of the chase, the excitement of a potential (or imagined) reward, is called *anticipatory joy*.

This anticipatory joy, which is prevalent in both animals and humans, helped us survive (through the pursuit of food sources) and ensured our reproduction as a species (through the pursuit of sexual partners). It is this anticipatory joy that makes hard-to-get partners so attractive, Black Friday sales so irresistible, Facebook "likes" so addictive, and the very latest iPhone so titillating. Whether it's for a trophy, a promotion, a slice at a popular pizza parlor, or Twitter followers, desire excites us. Anticipatory joy is why people go window-shopping, gamble, or test-drive Ferraris. Marketers are experts at tapping into our love of a good chase. They use techniques like special deals and unique or limited opportunities to entice us: "Don't miss out on the latest sale!" "Time-limited offer!" You may find that you too use these techniques in your business or negotiation endeavors.

Workaholism is really just another chase in disguise. Anticipatory joy drives work addiction—a tendency to work excessively and compulsively. Research[6] by Michael Treadway has shown that people who work hard release greater amounts of dopamine (neurotransmitters that are markers of pleasure) in reward areas of the brain. Overachievers live off the fleeting high that comes from responding to that one extra e-mail, getting that additional project out of the way, or checking one last thing off the to-do list. Work addiction—unlike addictions involving alcohol or other substances—is rewarded by our culture (with promotions, bonuses, praise, awards, and so on) and therefore considered a good thing despite its long-term negative impact on well-being.[7]

The "chase" mentality is pervasive in our culture because we are arguably facing the most difficult time in human history to resist external stimuli. Why? Technology allows work and personal demands to be on our radar all the time. Thanks to computers, smartphones, and tablets, the boss's latest request is sitting in an in-box, to-do lists reminders pop up on screens, and text requests pop up on phones. We don't even have to make the effort to check these devices; our smartphone or Apple watches will beep or buzz to notify us of incoming mail or messages. In addition, we spend time on social media—LinkedIn, Facebook, Twitter—to stay on top of the latest news and connected to our network.

Harvard Business School professor Leslie Perlow, author of *Sleeping with Your Smartphone,* calls people who can't let go of their work "successaholics" because she believes people become addicted to achievement. They suffer from what is well described by the slang acronym *FOMO: fear of missing out.* They need to always be "on" just in case—to ensure that they are on top of everything and that they master the next project or get the next deal. "We're obsessed with work because of the satisfaction we get from the kudos for achievement, not because of some deep-seated satisfaction from working long hours, as an end in itself," she notes in a *Harvard Business Review* article.[8] She points out that successaholics are, sadly, also the ones working on their phones and responding to e-mail instead of watching their infants grow or enjoying their best friend's wedding.

Given our propensity for anticipatory joy and the compulsion for the chase, it is no surprise that we are driven to get more and more things done, piling up achievements and accomplishments for some possible future success.

Unbeknownst to us, however, this constant focus on productivity actually hurts—rather than helps—our chances of success.

WHY CHASING THE FUTURE DOES NOT LEAD TO SUCCESS

The reason we are so hooked on getting things done is that we believe the payoff that comes from achievements—an award or a larger savings account—will ultimately lead to the biggest payoff of all: happiness. We have the illusion that the success, fame, money—fill in the blank—that we are chasing will bring us some kind of lasting fulfillment. We often expect that we'll be happy when we get this or that project over with. For example, you might think that if you work like a maniac, you'll get a sought-after promotion with a big raise, which will ease your financial anxieties at home, and once that anxiety is gone . . . well, you'll finally be happy.

However, even when people achieve their goals, the payoff for which they endured all the stress, anxiety, and health repercussions that result from overworking is fleeting. Dan Gilbert[9] at Harvard has shown that we are terrible at predicting what will or will not make us happy. We often overestimate the happiness something will bring us. Just like a cat who chases a toy but loses interest as soon as he catches it, when we finally get what we want—receiving a big end-of-year bonus, finding the perfect job, or even winning the lottery—we often find that we are not as happy as we thought we would be.[10]

Our future-oriented focus does of course have its benefits. Forward planning is not only wise but even essential in many domains of life, from professional development to personal finances. We need to think ahead, and some anxiety ("How can I make sure that our team successfully delivers our product to customers on time?" "How will I pay my mortgage?") comes with the territory. Research shows that thinking about the future can help you make wiser decisions overall,[11] including financial decisions like how much money goes in your savings account.[12]

Anticipatory joy in turn provides us with the determination, excitement, and grit needed to work hard for a promotion or new business deal, to complete marathons or graduate school degrees, or to gain fluency in a foreign language. We enjoy chasing our dreams and value things more if we worked hard to get them.

However, there are major problems with *constantly* trying to get things done and focusing on the next thing: doing so ironically prevents you from being as successful as you want to be and wreaks havoc on body and mind. Many studies[13] show that the workaholic or successaholic chase can be detrimental on a number of levels:

- **Health.** It is linked to lower levels of physical and psychological health. In particular, it is associated with burnout, emotional exhaustion, cynicism, and depersonalization (a disturbing sense of dissociation from yourself that accompanies prolonged stress or trauma). It is also linked to lower overall life satisfaction.[14]

- **Work.** It can—counterintuitively perhaps—damage productivity and performance. It has been linked to lower job satisfaction and increased job stress, which reduce productivity[15] by, for example, reducing attention span.[16] This should come as no surprise. If you are continuously focused on the next thing you need to accomplish, only part of your attention is directed toward your present activity.

- **Relationships.** At work, constantly focusing on achievement can increase negative interactions with co-workers, leading to competitiveness, rivalry, and distrust, which further lead to counterproductive work behaviors.[17] In personal relationships, it is linked to higher levels of work-life conflict, reduced family satisfaction and functioning, and relationship problems with spouses.[18] If you are always thinking about the next thing you want to accomplish, you likely are not as present for your family and loved ones. They inevitably sense that they are not as important as whatever task you are worried about tackling next.

From the outside we may look like we have it all, but on the inside, we are burned out, not performing to our highest level, and feeling miserable both emotionally and physically while our relationships suffer.

THE BENEFITS OF LIVING IN THE PRESENT

Paradoxically, slowing down and focusing on what is happening in front of you right now—being present instead of always having your mind on the next thing—will make you much more successful. Expressions like "live in the moment" or "carpe diem" sound like clichés, yet science backs them up robustly. Research shows that remaining present—rather than constantly focusing on what you have to do next—will make you more productive and happier and, moreover, will give you that elusive quality we attribute to the most successful people: charisma.

BEING PRESENT MAKES YOU MORE
PRODUCTIVE AND HAPPIER

Most of us have lost the simple ability to stay in the present. We maintain a packed schedule with hardly any breaks and fill every moment of down time with multitasking. For example, we take our children to the park after work while fitting in a call to a colleague; we attend a meeting while working on our to-do list for the following day; or we post a LinkedIn update as we are having lunch with a friend. When multitasking, we are never fully attentive to what is going on right now—and we lose out on what is happening in that precise moment.

Given the demands of this day and age and the pervasiveness of technology, you inevitably experience multiple personal and professional demands at any one time: you may be in a meeting at work but also watching for incoming texts from your spouse, who needs a ride home, or you may be finishing a work document while also keeping an eye on e-mails so you can respond to a client right away. Some workplaces expect you to be on top of your in-box at all times of the day. Even when there is no urgency involved, multitasking has become a way of life. You have become used to checking your phone while working, while spending time with your family, and even at the gym and during vacations.

Multitasking, instead of helping us accomplish more things faster, actually keeps us from doing anything well. When you are performing any individual task, if you are able to give it your undivided attention, you will accomplish it far more efficiently and quickly while also enjoying the process.

When we are doing several things at once, we cannot deeply process the material we are working on. Research shows that multitasking harms your memory. In one study, university students who had their laptops open during a lecture ended up scoring worse on traditional memory tests for lecture content than students who had their laptops closed.[19] Research also shows that our concentration skills weaken because we lose our ability to filter out unnecessary information and are therefore constantly thinking about other things.[20] In a sense, we've trained our brain to process several things at once, but the result is that nothing is processed well. One study showed that if you are driving and listening to someone speak at the same time, the brain activation otherwise devoted to driving decreases by 37 percent.[21] In other words, multitasking may mean doing more things but doing them less well. A manager at a communications firm told me that many of her employees are so focused on multitasking that they end up handing in subpar work. She finds herself telling her employees to slow down—an unusual request from a manager—because she knows that if they are present and deliberately thinking through each task, they would not only perform better but also learn from each task and thereby improve future performance as well.

When we are caught up in multitasking or preoccupied with the next thing we need to cross off the to-do list, not only are we harming our performance, we may also be harming our well-being. One study found that, the more people engaged in media multitasking (from word processing to text messaging and e-mail), the higher their anxiety and depression levels tended to be.[22] If you are constantly being pulled in several different directions, it is only natural that you will feel more stressed and overwhelmed.

On the other hand, research[23] shows that when we are completely in tune with what we are doing, we more fully enjoy that activity. Moreover, being completely present allows us to enter a state of complete absorption that is extremely productive. Think of a time when you were faced with a project you were dreading. You knew it would involve a lot of effort; maybe you kept putting it off. However, once you started— perhaps finally egged on by an impending deadline—you became engaged and the project just flowed. You found that you actually enjoyed the process. You became highly productive because you focused completely on the task at hand. Instead of being stressed about the future and having your attention pulled in different directions, you got the work done and done well, and you were happy to boot.

Research[24] by Mihály Csíkszentmihályi suggests that when you are completely immersed in an activity, you experience a highly energized and pure state of joy he calls *flow*. Flow occurs when you are 100 percent involved in an activity that is challenging enough to engage you (but not so challenging that it would take days to figure out). It is a state in which you are fully in the present moment, and it produces great pleasure. You often lose awareness of everything other than your activity. Your mind is completely and utterly absorbed. You are in the moment and things just seem to, well, flow. Those experiences of presence are deeply fulfilling because you are engaged, mind and body, in your experience.

There was a time when I couldn't stand running errands: getting gas, taking my car for an oil change, calling the electricity company about a bill, or going grocery shopping. Taking care of this or that silly errand instead of being "productive"— doing things that would serve some future goal like advancing my career—felt like a waste of time. I even looked for ways to outsource my errands. Eventually I realized that by constantly being in a "productive" mind-set, I was not only wearing myself out chasing that next goal, but I was missing out on the people and opportunities around me. My life was actually going on right there and then, but I was missing it. I would meet a friend I hadn't seen for a long time but couldn't be present because I had to check my e-mail to find out if I had missed something, or I would go home early to "get things done." In reality, I was living in constant anxiety . . . with my mind constantly wrapped up in the future.

I stopped running a million miles an hour after I had gall bladder surgery. I was forced to do nothing for two weeks. I had no choice in the matter. To my surprise, despite the intense physical pain, life instantly became a hundred times more pleasurable. It was as if I were soaking in the sun around me. The food tasted so much better, my rest was deep, and incredible joy stirred within me for no reason. What was going on? Would I need to be on vacation for the rest of my life? No, it wasn't the fact that I was on leave from work. It was that I was on leave from my own internal taskmaster. As a consequence, I could be present, really present, with what I had. And I realized I had missed out on the immense joy of daily activities, social interactions, and time spent appreciating my environment. Interestingly, when I went back to work, I found that I was more present with my activities and co-workers, and as a consequence, I got more accomplished—and far more efficiently than when my mind was preoccupied with thoughts about the future.

Yet many of us miss out on this incredible experience of productivity and happiness for much of our lives. According to a study[25] of five thousand people by Matthew Killingsworth and Daniel Gilbert of Harvard University, adults spend only about 50 percent of their time in the present moment. In other words, we are mentally checked out half of the time we spend working, being with friends and family, or engaging in activities we would usually enjoy. We are absorbed in a myriad of other things beyond what is happening right now.

In addition to measuring when people's minds were wandering, the scientists also collected information on happiness levels. They found that when we are in the present moment (that is, thinking about the activity we are doing), we are also at our happiest, no matter what we are doing. In other words, even if you are engaging in an activity you usually find unpleasant (for instance, filling out administrative paperwork), you are happier when you are one hundred percent consumed in that activity than when you are thinking about something else while doing so. Accordingly, Killingsworth and Gilbert titled their scientific paper "A Wandering Mind Is an Unhappy Mind."

Other studies have confirmed that, in general, a wandering mind is associated with a negative mood.[26] When your mind is caught up in the past or future, chances are you experience negative emotions. Anxiety and fear, for example, arise when your mind is focused on the future. In particular, when you are focused on how much you still need to accomplish, you typically experience anxiety and stress. As for negative states like anger or frustration, you'll notice that they arise when your mind is caught in the past; whatever happened to make you angry is over, yet your mind is still dwelling on that event. Regret also has to do with the past. It's a new day, a new hour, and a new circumstance, but you're still wallowing in a situation you wish you had handled differently.

I'm certainly not saying that we shouldn't daydream or reminisce; as we will see in chapter 4, we absolutely should set time aside for such activities since they fuel our creativity. Daydreaming about wonderful future events can lead to creative thoughts and more positive emotions. You can also derive joy from reliving a happy memory or musing on a particularly interesting topic.[27] However, as Killingsworth and Gilbert show, when we are engaged in a task, we are happiest and most productive when we are completely attentive to it.

Why does the present makes us happy? Because we fully experience the things going on around us. Instead of getting caught up in a race to accomplish more things faster, we slow down and are actually *with* the people we are with, *immersed* in the ideas being discussed, and *fully engaged* in our projects.

We all have available choices that can help us stay present in our tasks. Clear your desk of distractions, put your cell phone on silent, use programs like Focus to block websites that you use to procrastinate (such as social media websites), and log off e-mail. Set a timer to make sure you stay with the task at hand until a certain time. I like to use an old-school hourglass.

BEING PRESENT INCREASES YOUR CHARISMA

If you meet someone at a cocktail party whose eyes are constantly flitting around the room, do they make a good impression? Do they appear magnetic or charming? Probably not. Their mind is clearly somewhere else—maybe trying to figure out if there is someone in the room who is more important than you. They are not focusing on the conversation, and they may glance at (or even focus on) their mobile devices. Are you likely to want to speak to them again? Chances are you will not. No one is interested in talking to someone who is not present. Worse yet is if they are not present *and* they are focused on technology. One research study[28] showed that the mere presence of a cell phone impaired the sense of connection in a face-to-face conversation.

However, if you meet someone who is completely attentive to you and actively engaged in the conversation, you are much more likely to find them likable and interesting. If that person's cell phone rings without them checking it, they get double brownie points. Why? Because in that moment, the only thing that seems to matter to them is *you.* You are the most important person there, and they have gifted you all of their attention at that moment.

A charismatic person is able to exert significant influence because he or she connects with others in meaningful ways.[29] It's no surprise that highly charismatic people—US presidents are a frequent example—are often described as having the ability to make you feel as if you were the only person in the room. Given how rare it is to receive that kind of attention from anyone, the ability to be fully present makes a big impression.

We often think of charisma as a special gift—the *je ne sais quoi* that makes someone starlike. Max Weber defined charisma as "a certain quality of an individual personality by virtue of which he is set apart from ordinary men and treated as endowed with supernatural, superhuman, or at least specifically exceptional powers or qualities. These are . . . not accessible to the ordinary person, but are regarded as of divine origin or as exemplary, and on the basis of them the individual concerned is treated as a leader."[30]

While research on charisma is still in development, one of the most extensive studies on charisma[31] found that charisma is not so much a gift as a learnable skill that has a lot to do with the ability to be *fully present*. The study pointed to six elements of a charismatic person:

1. **Empathy**—the ability to see things from another person's perspective and to understand how that person is feeling. You can only be empathic and place yourself in another person's shoes if you are fully attentive to them —which you are obviously only able to do if you are completely present with them.

2. **Good listening skills**—the ability to truly hear what someone is trying to communicate to you, both verbally and nonverbally. Think of the person at the conference social hour who interrupts you or can't wait to interject her two cents. She is not truly listening to you because she's thinking about herself—what she will say, how smart she will sound, how impressed you will be. If you are distracted or thinking about what to say next—not truly present—you are not truly listening.

3. **Eye contact**—the ability to meet and maintain someone's gaze. Eye contact is one of the most powerful forms of human connection.[32] We intuitively feel that when someone's gaze shifts away from us, their attention has also shifted away from us. And this intuition is backed up by neuroscience research,[33] which has found that the same brain regions are used when your gaze wanders as when your mind wanders. When you are present and looking someone in the eye, the impact of that connection can

be powerful. In addition to feeling *heard,* because of your empathy and good listening skills, people actually feel *seen.*

4. **Enthusiasm**—the ability to uplift another person through praise of their actions or ideas. Enthusiasm is difficult to fake because it is such an authentic emotion. It can only occur when you sincerely engage with what someone else is doing or saying. For your enthusiasm to come across powerfully, you have to sincerely feel it. Again, your ability to be fully present and engaged is essential.

5. **Self-confidence**—the ability to act authentically and with assurance without worrying about what other people think. Many people are so busy worrying about how they appear that they end up coming across as nervous or inauthentic. Their focus is on themselves rather than on the other person. When you are fully present, you are focused on others rather than yourself. As a consequence, you naturally come across as confident: instead of worrying about what others are thinking of you, you are composed, genuine, and natural.

6. **Skillful speaking**—the ability to profoundly connect with others. It is essential to *know* your audience if you want to make an impact. The only way to do so, however, is to tune in to them. When you are one hundred percent present with your audience, you are able to understand where they are coming from and how they are interpreting your words. Only then can your words be sensitive and appropriate. When you speak skillfully, you will be truly heard.

Charisma, simply put, is absolute presence.

While constantly focusing on the next thing or the next person may seem productive, slowing down and being present has far more profound benefits. By being present, you will enter a state of flow that is highly productive and will become more charismatic, making people around you feel understood and supported. You will have good relationships, which are one of the biggest predictors of success[34] and happiness.[35]

HOW TO BRING YOUR MIND
INTO THE PRESENT

Given Killingsworth and Gilbert's findings that the mind wanders 50 percent of the time, bringing our mind back into the present can seem daunting. Let's face it—it won't be easy to undo a habit we have had for years. However, the first step is awareness.

When you notice that your mind is going toward future-oriented thoughts, you can choose not to follow the train of thought—instead, you *can* nudge your mind back into the present. Let's say you are working at your desk, playing with your child, or having dinner with your spouse, and you notice that your mind is somewhere else. Of course, this isn't the first time your mind has wandered away from the present, but when you first consciously observe this pattern, it can be a little disturbing. You might have thoughts like "Wow, here I am with my loved ones and I can't focus on them." But this awareness is key. Try reorienting your attention fully on what is going on in front of you. This exercise is not easy at first, but, like working a muscle, you can strengthen your ability to stay present by repeating this exercise. Like learning a sport, it takes training. The following exercises, when done regularly, can help you be present more easily.

Practice consciously being present. Start with a ten-minute exercise. For example, if you have a Powerpoint presentation to prepare or are working on filing your taxes, experiences you dislike or want to get over with as fast as possible, see if you can give them your full attention instead. Use these otherwise tedious activities as great opportunities to train your attention. You may find that you even start to enjoy them. Notice when you get the itch to distract yourself by surfing the Internet or checking your phone and practice focusing exclusively on the task at hand.

Outside of work, take time to watch the sunset, brush your pet, or do your errands without texting, talking on the phone, or occupying yourself with planning at the same time. The more you practice being present with your activities, the more being present becomes a habit. It's not about how quickly you chop the vegetables or how soon you can get dinner put together. It's about the act of chopping itself: find pleasure in cutting the vegetables evenly, for example. Notice every detail.

Meditate. In 2012, a reported 18 million Americans practiced meditation[36]—that's 8 percent of the population! This number has probably risen since then, considering the growing mindfulness movement and a large body of supportive research studies. Meditation—discussed at greater length in chapter 3—can help you cultivate a state of calm and quiet in your mind, displacing the cycle of desire and anxiety that comes with chasing the future. Research[37] shows that experienced meditators have less brain activity in areas related to mind-wandering.

I have taught meditation to students, professionals, and veterans for years. Often, right after a meditation, people say, "The colors look so much brighter in the room." It's not that the meditation somehow enhanced their vision—to my knowledge there is no research showing that effect. What happens, however, is that their minds settle down, and as a result, they become more present and therefore attentive to their environment. Before, as they came into the room, their vision was obscured by a barrage of thoughts.

There are many forms of meditation. Find the one that is right for you. If you are not drawn to meditation as a way of calming down and centering yourself, there are other activities, such as yoga, yoga-based breathing exercises, tai chi, or walking quietly in nature, that can help settle your thoughts. I have personally found—and preliminary research also shows—that *abhyanga* ayurvedic oil self-massage is a powerful way to quiet the mind.[38] Find the activity that allows you to settle your mind, your thoughts, your emotions, and your desires, so that you become grounded in the here and now.

Breath Focus. An age-old and effective practice for bringing the mind back into the present is to focus your attention on one thing, for example on your breath. When you find your mind wandering, take a deep breath in; as you breathe out, let go of your thoughts—as if you were consciously exhaling them—and bring your attention back to the present. You may have to do this exercise repeatedly, whenever you become caught up in a flurry of thoughts.

Another breathing exercise that research shows helps strengthen your attention is breath-counting. Count each breath you take, and when you reach ten, start over. While this exercise may not sound very exciting, research[39] shows that it increases your ability to pay attention and stay in the present moment.

Truly experience pleasure. Here's a fun one. When you feel pleasure, close your eyes and be one hundred percent present with that pleasure. Whether it is emotional (such as love) or sensual (food or touch or sound), savor the sensation or experience completely. Instead of reading while you eat, savor your food, for example. Research[40] shows that learning to bask in your pleasurable experiences helps to extend the feeling. Not only will you enjoy pleasurable experiences all the more, you may have fewer cravings for more because your experiences are more satisfying.

Take a technology fast. Evan Price, the founder of Pinterest, understands the importance of unplugging. He told the *New York Times* that he enjoys going on such long drives with his wife that he loses cell phone signal.[41] One of the greatest exercises in presence and joy is to spend a half day or whole day on a technology fast, ideally in nature, without a schedule. Let your mind rest and relax. Take aimless walks. Contemplate the sky. This may feel strange at first, and you may even start to be antsy or anxious because you are unaccustomed to not "doing" anything. It may even make you uncomfortable (after all, one study shows that people would rather give themselves electric shocks than sit in a room by themselves doing nothing!),[42] but see if you can move past that state. It's just a phase. When my husband and I visited an electricity-free, Wi-Fi-free resort in a bird sanctuary in Mexico, we were thrilled to be completely unplugged from the world. Yet despite the ocean sounds and flocks of flamingos outside our window, it still took us at least three days to really adjust to being completely present. The mind takes some time to settle down.

You can learn to relax your mind. The quality of your life and work depends on it.

A famous parable recounts how a successful and wealthy investment banker tries to encourage a humble Mexican man fishing on a pier to boost his output so he can make more money, grow his business, and eventually become a millionaire. The fisherman asks, "What for?" To which the banker says, "So you can retire, relax, and just fish"—which is precisely what the fisherman was doing in the first place. This parable illustrates how you can get so caught up in the chase that you forget your end goal, which is to be happy.

Being ambitious and having goals are of course essential. However, to actually achieve those goals to the best of your ability, remain present. Being present allows you to find fulfillment in the moment, in the task at hand—rather than in some distant future, after you have achieved everything and ticked every last task off of your list. When you slow down and focus one hundred percent on the tasks you are working on or the people you are with, then everything becomes joyful, even the mundane. That joy in turn leads you to perform better, be more productive, become charismatic, and build better relationships.

After taking our happiness class and subsequently learning to meditate, Jackie Rotman began to consciously live in the present moment. She ended up doing extremely well at Stanford and was arguably one of the most popular students in her cohort. Unlike many students who were stressed out, holed up in their rooms and exclusively thinking about achievement, Jackie focused on the tasks at hand. She enjoyed her time and was glowing and happy. As a consequence of her infectious joy, she had a remarkable ability to connect with people and make friends. The relationships she had and the friendships she built significantly helped develop her postgraduation career.

As Jackie's story shows, being fully present requires a shift in our attention—a shift that might be quite difficult at first but whose effect on our well-being and success is well worth the effort.

TWO

STEP OUT OF OVERDRIVE

TAP INTO YOUR NATURAL RESILIENCE

> Feelings come and go like clouds in a windy
> sky. Conscious breathing is my anchor.
> —*Thich Nhat Hanh*

In March 2011, António Horta-Osório, a young star in the finance world, was appointed to become the youngest of Britain's Big Five bank CEOs, heading Lloyds Banking Group. His arrival on the scene led to tremendous hope for Lloyds—which was facing a substantial number of problems. António worked tirelessly, often logging marathon ninety-hour weeks to turn the bank around.[1]

Everyone wants to be successful. What success looks like, of course, is up to you—a rock star, a skilled dancer, a fabulous cook, a celebrity personal trainer, CEO of your own company, or the best parent of your children. The point is, we all want to live at our full potential. When it comes to our goals, dreams, and aspirations, no one wants to be below average. And one of the things we've learned is that we need to have *drive*. Drive, ambition, motivation, go-getterness, hunger— call it what you want.

Whether we find it in our employees, our family members, or ourselves, we think of drive as a highly desirable trait. We are constantly trying to do more and be better: advance in our professions, lose weight, make more money, increase our athleticism, become perfect parents. Drive is a positive thing—in *doses*. The problem is that we are living in *over*drive, and both science and our own personal experiences are showing us that we are paying a high price for it: chronic stress.

Stress can be defined as having to face an enormous challenge while feeling that you have too few resources to meet that challenge. Historically, humans have lived under enormous challenges. Famine, wars, disease, natural disasters, and high infant mortality were mainstays for centuries. Today, however, most of us no longer have to contend with these stressors. However, our stress levels remain extraordinarily high. According to the American Institute of Stress, a survey taken from a representative sample of Americans in 2014 shows these statistics:

- Annual stress-related health-care costs for employers: $300 billion
- Percent of people who regularly experience physical costs caused by stress: 77
- Percent of people who regularly experience psychological costs of stress: 73
- Percent of people who report lying awake at night due to stress: 48[2]

Given that these statistics come from 2014, a time when most Americans lived in relatively safe environments and had basic needs (food and shelter) taken care of, the numbers are alarming. What is more, 48 percent felt that their stress had increased over the past five years, suggesting that stress levels are on the rise.

Eight months after António Horta-Osório took on the high-power, high-pressure CEO position at Lloyds, he took a medical leave of absence due to extreme stress and fatigue. His stress was so high that he was unable to sleep for five days running.[3] When the news of his leave of absence hit, Lloyds lost £1 billion in market value. As in António Horta-Osório's case, overdrive can ironically backfire and prevent us from achieving our goals.

We have come to accept that we can't succeed without living in overdrive; that we can't succeed without stress. Yet we are mistaken. Research shows that stress actually stops us from being as successful as we could be. There is a better way: fostering resilience.

WHY WE EQUATE SUCCESS WITH STRESS

Where do we get this notion that stress is both an essential requirement for and an inevitable by-product of success? Our culture idealizes professions that involve high pressure—from TV shows about emergency room doctors working in the most intense situations and busy lawyers running from case to case, to books and articles celebrating extraordinary CEOs and entrepreneurs who run major companies, volunteering on boards for charitable causes, and still managing to help their kids with homework.

Our culture also values persevering to attain our goals, and fighting to outperform others—all of which involve some form of stress. The idea of being a go-getter involves straining, pushing, and competing. When people successfully complete a project, reach a goal, or master a feat, the slang expressions to congratulate them are "you killed it" or "you destroyed it"; forcefulness is part of our understanding of success. As a consequence, we value intensity, which inherently involves physiological stress.

In fact, success is popularly equated with aggressiveness. Research[4] I conducted at Stanford with psychology professor Jeanne Tsai shows that, in the United States, when we are in a situation in which we want to influence others, we value high-intensity positive emotions like excitement (as opposed to low-intensity emotions like calm). Why? Because we believe such emotions will make us more influential. In a study in which we assigned participants to be either leaders or followers, we found that those in leadership roles automatically wanted to feel more high-intensity positive emotions. However, emotions like excitement—despite being positive—activate our physiology's stress response due to their intensity. In other words, even the positive emotions that we want to feel in order to be successful are inherently stress-inducing and taxing on the body.

The idea that stress and success are inevitably intertwined has become so ingrained in our culture and work habits that we take pride in our stress levels. We brag about how much we have on our plates or the length of our to-do lists. We boast about the craziness of our schedules. We advertise how little sleep we've gotten and that we haven't taken a vacation in years. We may not like to feel stressed, but we wear it like a badge of honor. We seem to think that the more stress we experience—and hopefully endure—the more successful we will be.

Science shows that this drive-and-stress theory of success—though so widely accepted—backfires in the long run. Stress in small doses or spurts can help us perform at our best and might even help us achieve a short-term goal. Because of this positive effect, many people feel that stress has worked for them in the past, and therefore they conclude it's necessary all the time. However, over time, chronic stress is the number one enemy of success. It depletes us and weakens the cognitive skills we most need. As we saw in the story of António Horta-Osório, far from helping us accomplish more, it can be a major obstacle.

GOOD STRESS, BAD STRESS, AND SUCCESS

Stress is not all bad, of course. Short-term stress serves the purpose of fueling us. Think of the adrenaline rush that gets you across the road quickly when you see an oncoming car. A little momentary stress can also be good for your health.[5] In a series of landmark studies, Firdaus Dhabhar, a colleague and professor of psychiatry at Stanford University, discovered that stress can provide great physiological and psychological benefits, including enhanced immunity.[6] He was the first to suggest that the biology of a short-term stress response could be harnessed to increase protection and performance.[7] In a well-cited and groundbreaking study, Firdaus demonstrated the potentially pro tective effects of short-term stress and the harmful effects of chronic stress.[8]

Right before I underwent gallbladder surgery, Firdaus reminded me that my stress response would help in the healing process by strengthening the immune system, provided I kept my stress levels low *before* the surgery. As shown in a study from his research group,[9] surgery triggers a stress response, flooding the body with chemicals to hasten healing.[10] However, if I entered surgery chronically stressed, my immune response would actually be weaker because I would have already diminished my body's resources. (I ended up attending a two-day silent meditation retreat immediately before the surgery and healed very well!)

Short-term stress can provide additional benefits. For example, short-term stress can lead to better mental and physical performance,[11] especially when an individual is skilled in the task at hand—for instance, public speaking, a bicycle race, or a musical performance. However, this is the case only if the individual is not suffering from chronic stress. The Yerkes-Dodson Law[12]—named after the two researchers who discovered it—stipulates that, like an inverted Ushaped curve, a certain level of stress helps us perform better, but once it gets too high, it actually gets in our way. For example, if you are adept at giving professional presentations, a little stress may help you do great, whereas too much impedes your performance.

Other studies show that in some situations, stress can facilitate bonding, creating a support system around you.[13] Acute stress can increase cooperative, social, and friendly behavior. This positive social response could help explain the human connection that occurs during crises or natural catastrophes—think about New York City after 9/11. This connection may be partly responsible for our collective survival as a species.

But we can have too much of a good thing. You have probably read about the negative effects of chronic stress. Stress in large quantities and over long periods will damage your health,[14] your relationships, and your work. And as we saw with António Horta-Osório of Lloyds Banking Group, it can have a dramatic effect on the performance— and ultimately, the success—of the organization for which you work.

Scientific research overwhelmingly shows that chronic stress makes you more prone to illness[15] and inflammation,[16] and even accelerates cellular aging.[17] It can also decrease productivity by impairing your cognitive abilities. Have you found that you have problems remembering things under high stress? Stress maintained over long periods harms your memory in particular[18] but also your ability to be creative, to see situations clearly, to think outside the box, to problem-solve skillfully, and to make good decisions.[19] There's even evidence that chronic stress makes you a terrible manager and leader. Stress has a ripple effect, increasing the stress of those around you. Anxious emotions, such as fear, are physiologically contagious through pheromones, chemicals released in our sweat. When someone emits "fear pheromones," the people who come into contact with that person show greater activation in brain areas corresponding to anxiety and fear (particularly the amygdala).[20] And we don't need research to tell us that when we bring stress home to our families, the results are equally disastrous.

Since not all stress is bad, the trick is to harness the benefits of short-term stress while not falling prey to chronic stress. In other words, sustainable long-term success is not about burning the candle at both ends; it is about learning to skillfully surf the stress wave. And even though intense stress can knock us out, we can also recover from its depleting effect.

To do that, we turn to resilience—our ability to quickly recover from stressful situations or setbacks—which is fortunately as natural to our physiology as the stress response. Can we be buoyant no matter how rough the waters? Can we find the drive and energy to accomplish our goals without the exhaustion and anxiety of chronic stress? The answer is yes. However, while most people know very well how to get stressed, fewer know how to tap into their own built-in reservoir of resilience. The good news is that you can easily learn to do so.

OUR NATURAL RESILIENCE

Resilience is the ability to quickly bounce back from the stressful situations you face every day: a difficult interaction with someone, a delayed flight that threatens to make you late for an important sales call, working long hours on a project with a looming deadline, and so on.

We have all learned about the fight-or-flight response, where our bodies—in fact, the bodies of most animals—prepare to either fight off a potentially deadly attack or run away. However, what most of us have not learned is what happens after the threat has passed and our bodies return to their normal state—the rest-and-digest response.

Consider a lion chasing an antelope in the wild, with the antelope in flight mode, sympathetic nervous system fully activated and adrenalin pumping. If the lion catches her, her life ends right there. But if she escapes, once out of harm's way, the antelope's stress is over almost immediately. The parasympathetic nervous system, which is responsible for "resting and digesting," will kick in, and she will peacefully relax and return to grazing in the sun. The fight-or-flight state has placed tremendous demands on her physiology, but as soon as it is deactivated she can focus on recovering and regaining her full strength. Within minutes, therefore, her nervous system has calmed down to allow her to regain an optimal state in which she can restore her resources and energy.

The key to her resilience is her ability

- to quickly return to the restorative rest-and-digest state;
- to remain in that state until an extreme life-threatening situation taxes her again;
- to overcome the next challenge at full strength.

Animals running for their lives in the wild are not the only ones that experience remarkable resilience in the face of a threat or stress. Take your dog to the veterinarian and you'll notice a huge stress response—he might start shaking, lowering his ears, and pulling on the leash to resist going into the exam room. However, that stress response subsides quickly once the exam is over and your pet is back in the comfort and familiarity of your home. You can even observe resilience in kids. Children who go through a stressful episode, such as a first day of school, bounce back immediately. They may be emotional while they say good-bye to their parents, but the emotions often last minutes, and soon they are smiling again.

The fact that children and animals recover so quickly from stress shows just how naturally resilient our nervous system is. We are meant to return to a state of well-being quickly and effortlessly.

So why is it that, as adults, we often seem to have a hard time handling stress and bouncing back? We have somehow lost our natural resilience. Think about it: how quickly do you bounce back from frustrations, stressful episodes, and disagreements? Five minutes? An hour? One day? Five days? Do you still feel stress's pinch at the very thought of them? We can receive one disturbing call and feel angry all day about it. Maybe even all week or month. Many people go to their graves harboring anger from an event that happened decades ago!

Many adults, it seems, have simply forgotten how to tap into their natural resilience. There are a couple of reasons for this phenomenon. First, there are biological reasons why we still worry even when we don't have threats looming over us. Second, resilience is neglected in our current culture.

RESILIENCE SABOTEURS

What prevents adults from enjoying the resilience children—and even animals—seem to tap into so easily? Why does our stress linger so much longer than theirs, sometimes becoming chronic?

The answer is in our brain. Our capacity for thought—as precious as it is—gets in our way. In addition to a fretful mind, popular messages encourage us to live in overdrive, making it all the more difficult for us to return to a calm state. Let's examine each of these resilience saboteurs.

OUR MINDS

We share many similar brain regions with animals: for example, regions responsible for sight, balance, and fear. Unlike most animals, however, we have an especially well-developed neocortex, which gives us the capacity to have an intellect and to reflect. Thank goodness for our neocortex—it is a beautiful gift that allows us to have insight, to develop language, to read this book, and to communicate thoughts, ideas, and feelings. Unfortunately, it also gives us the ability to worry, despair, perseverate (psychology lingo for "rehash the same thing over and over again"), imagine the worst, dramatize, and create fictitious scenarios and totally wild interpretations.

If the antelope were graced with a neocortex like ours, she might not relax quite so fast after the stressful episode with the lion. Instead, she might replay the scenario in her mind over and over again, worry and plan excape scenarios in case the lion returns, develop insomnia obsessing over the idea that the lion could potentially harm her baby, and so on.

Does this sound familiar?

Our brains tend to focus on negative thoughts more than positive ones.[21] Scientists hypothesize that this negativity bias is evolutionarily adaptive. By remembering dangerous encounters with predators, for example, our ancestors were more likely to steer clear of them. However, nowadays this tendency is no longer necessary and often gets in our way.

With just one or two negative thoughts, you can agitate your physiology to extremes. As Dr. Paul Gilbert,[22] a British psychologist and founder of Compassion-Focused Therapy, points out, it only takes a call from a frustrated boss, an angry text message from a romantic partner or friend, or even a curse from a stranger to immediately whip your entire physiological chemistry into an anxious state. And it's exhausting. Given the number of stressful situations we encounter and the angry or anxious thoughts they generate, this response can prevent us from resting and restoring ourselves.

Even opening our in-box is enough to assail us with stressors. Research shows that the more you check your e-mail, the more stress you experience.[23] The reverse is also true. A study[24] out of the University of California, Irvine, by Gloria Mark and US Army researcher Armand

Cadello investigated the impact of e-mail on work productivity and stress levels. When e-mail was removed, participants in the study noticed an improved ability to focus on the task at hand. They also found that stress, as measured by heart rate, was lower without e-mail.

This should come as no surprise. E-mails are stripped of social cues. Communication was undoubtedly more empathic and less stress-inducing before e-mail—people talked on the phone or in person, allowing for greater adjustment of interactions based on social cues. For example, if someone looked visibly fatigued or unwell, their supervisor may not have been as hard on them. Sadly, those cues are not present with e-mail, and immediate responses are often expected. All we receive is a written message whose tone is difficult to interpret. A short e-mail from your boss might sound angry and make you nervous. An emotional e-mail from your partner might completely upset your focus at work as you worry about what it might mean. An e-mail disclosing new information about an impending legal matter can further increase your anxiety.

How does it feel to receive dozens of such e-mails throughout the day? In our e-mail-less past, we would experience maybe one highly emotional event a day or two or three at the most (for example, a confrontation with a colleague, a spat with a spouse, or a phone call from an angry friend). In 2014, business users sent and received on average 121 e-mails a day (up from 105 in 2011, and expected to increase to 140 by 2018).[25] As a consequence, one hour of e-mail can take you through a huge range of emotions and stressors. Sure, you get e-mails that make you happy too—photos of your nephews, someone's marriage announcement—but unfortunately, we are more influenced by negative input because, as discussed earlier, the mind tends to focus on negative information.[26]

Is it any wonder that we come home feeling exhausted after a long day of doing nothing but sitting at our computer?

EXTERNAL AND INTERNAL STIMULI

Not only do our minds constantly produce thoughts that agitate us, but our nervous systems are perpetually overstimulated by external messages. Buy more stuff, look better, exercise more, eat better, perform at a higher level, learn more. The messages we receive—at school, at work, through advertising, and through cultural media like TV shows—push us harder and harder, grossly overstimulating us and triggering stress responses.

If you feel assailed, overwhelmed, or overstimulated by the many messages that come your way every day, there's a reason for that. Commercial and media organizations routinely employ stress-boosting techniques to capture our attention. As described earlier, our brain is wired to focus on fearful or negative stimuli more than positive ones.[27] That's why messages designed to incite fear and anxiety permeate our culture: anyone who wants to capture our attention knows how to assail us with these stressful stimuli. News agencies, for example, keep us hooked with negative headlines (war! conflict! death! destruction!). Even special offers and sales (think about Black Friday) manipulate our adrenaline system to ensure that we respond. As a result, we live in a daily state of stress. No matter how aware we are of these messaging techniques, we all feel at least some of their stressful effects.

To make matters worse, it's not just external messages that cause us stress. We ourselves play an active role in keeping our adrenaline levels high. To keep up with these cultural messages, we have learned how to activate our stress response daily. Although the stress response is meant for rare and life-threatening occasions, we call it up voluntarily. In fact, most people depend on it and use it just to meet the demands of the day. You may recognize that you purposefully call on it by overscheduling yourself, overcommitting and waiting until the last minute to complete projects—because you depend on anxiety to fuel yourself. When you are tired and really need to rest, you may find that you instead choose to keep pushing or relying on stimulants like coffee, sugar, or energy drinks to give you the "high" you need to keep going. In fact, a growing trend shows that students and professionals are engaging in the dangerous (not to mention addictive) habit of popping stimulant drugs designed to treat attention deficit disorder so as to stay up and focus for longer hours.[28] We have become hooked on the fast lane.

Is it surprising then that, when we come home at night, we're still buzzing from the day and can't relax and go to sleep? Overstimulated and unable to calm down, we turn to depressants like alcohol and sleeping pills or antianxiety medication to restore us. The constant back-and-forth between stimulant-induced anxiety and depressant-induced drowsiness further taxes our already exhausted nervous system.

In sum, every day, our thoughts as well as external messages and stimulants sabotage our ability to tap into our natural resilience. We then routinely try to manage this stress in ways that not only are ineffective but often make us even more anxious and depleted.

WHY STRESS MANAGEMENT BACKFIRES

Through our education and professions, we learn all kinds of information, life tools, and discipline —but we never learn how to properly respond to stress and difficulty. Instead, we try to talk ourselves out of the emotion, "tough it out," or reach for a drink. Research shows, however, that these approaches don't work and can even be destructive.

YOU CAN'T TALK YOURSELF OUT OF STRESS

Studies show that the way we perceive a situation can help us regulate our emotions to some extent, but when we find ourselves in difficult situations, talking ourselves out of feeling stressed is extremely challenging if not impossible.

For example, if after going shopping you return to your car to find a $30 parking ticket, you might be able to soothe yourself and calm your initial anxiety about receiving a ticket with thoughts of how grateful you are that your car was not towed or how happy you are that the designer suit you just bought was on sale—which made getting the ticket worth it.

But if you return to your parking spot to find that your car has been impounded, you'll have to pay a $750 fine to recover it, and you're late for an important job interview, it might just take all the strength you have to not lose it right there and then.

In a high-stress situation like this one, attempting to use thoughts to change your emotions is likely to be fruitless. Try to talk yourself into sleeping when you are anxious the night before a big interview or exam or performance. Better yet, think about how helpful it is when a friend or manager tells you to "just relax" when you are stressed. That's not only unhelpful, it's downright irritating.

Have you ever wished to forget an argument with someone, only to find yourself rehashing it in your head for hours? Why is it so hard to control our mind, especially when we are stressed? Daniel Wegner, a psychology professor at Harvard University, has shown in several studies that the intention to control a particular thought often breaks down under stress or mental overload and actually ends up triggering the unwanted thought, undermining our best intentions.[29] Wegner describes this as an "ironic process." When we resist a certain thought or action—trying not to eat junk food when on a diet, or trying not to think of someone you just broke up with—our efforts can easily backfire under stress.

TOUGHING IT OUT DOESN'T WORK

When we feel anxious and can't talk our way out of stressful thoughts, we often end up suppressing emotions. We put on a poker face and "suck it up." Research by Stanford psychologist James Gross demonstrates that attempting to suppress emotions (by not showing our emotion) leads to the opposite of what we want. By trying to hide emotions, we actually manifest them more strongly physiologically. For example, anger or stress increase the heart rate and make your palms sweat. Suppressing these emotions increases their physiological impact. In fact, it even impacts the physiology of whoever you are talking with by raising their heart level! Suppressing negative emotions on a regular basis actually makes people experience more negative emotions and less positive emotions.[30] Individuals who tend to suppress have lower self-esteem, optimism, and well-being and higher rates of depression as well as impaired memory. Suppression negatively impacts their relationships and social life.[31]

CHOCOLATE AND ALCOHOL AREN'T ANY BETTER

Instead of dealing with stress constructively, we often resort instead to compensatory substances like food, alcohol, and cigarettes, or distract ourselves by watching excessive TV, playing video games, or even working compulsively. However, the unhealthy habits we entertain in those moments often end up making us feel worse.

Expressions like "I need a drink" or "I need a smoke" have become so common that we even use them as a joke to refer to a rough situation we're in. Most of us have indulged in moments of weakness or exhaustion when the only thing we can think of to make us feel better is that extra sweet treat or glass of wine. And while they might give us a momentary feeling of relief, they obviously do not resolve the stress. And if resorted to often, they aggravate the stress of an already depleted nervous system.

You probably know your own weaknesses—the compensatory substances or habits that you rely on to cope with stress—and you may even feel bad about them. But you shouldn't. It's natural to seek ways to soothe and regulate ourselves. And for good reason: we intuitively know that, like the antelope that reverts to a state of calm, we too can reset our systems and return to a place of balance. The only difference is that we are seeking to restore balance the wrong way—by trying to talk ourselves out of it, by suppressing our feelings and by resorting to comfort food, drinks, and so on. We have so forgotten how to naturally return to a balanced state that Silicon Valley start-ups are creating wearable technologies designed to calm you down.[32]

TAPPING INTO NATURAL RESILIENCE

I work extensively with veterans who have suffered posttraumatic stress syndrome. In a particular session, one of the veterans told me, "I know I'm in the US and there's no danger inside the shopping mall, but I still have to brace myself for twenty minutes before I can walk in." This example demonstrates how powerless our thinking mind can be when we're in a highly anxious state. Despite *knowing* intellectually that the mall is not dangerous, this veteran *still* needed to brace himself physically for a long time before he could enter. Altering his thoughts was not enough for him to cope with intense stress. And it often isn't enough for us either, especially when we are under chronic stress.

If our thoughts and minds are not the best gateway to tap into resilience, what is? Our bodies. You have probably noticed that the state of your body affects your mind—too much caffeine can make you feel anxious, and hunger can make you feel grumpy. Similarly, if you can bring greater relaxation and ease into your body, your mind will naturally be at its best and have the chance to reset from the stress. Think of how you feel after a massage, a hike in nature, or a warm bath.

And yet when we need immediate help to deal with a difficult situation, we can't usually run a bath or get a massage. So what is the fastest way to achieve well-being? It is so close to you that it can easily be overlooked: your breath—a rapid and reliable pathway into your nervous system dedicated to helping you regain your optimal state.

Even if you have an intuitive understanding that the breath can regulate the mind and emotions—you probably have told someone who was stressed to "take a deep breath"—you might not be fully aware of its power.

Breathing is something we do every day, every moment. It's arguably the single most important action of our life. It is also the most neglected one, because it mostly happens on its own and below the level of our awareness. What makes breathing so unique is that it can happen automatically (like digestion and heartbeat), or it can be controlled through will. It is the one autonomic function you have a say over.

Indian humanitarian and spiritual leader Sri Sri Ravi Shankar has spent much of his life teaching yoga-based breathing practices around the world through his organization the Art of Living Foundation. He points out that "our first act in this world is to take a deep breath in, and our last act will be taking a deep breath out. Breathing is life. Yet, we are typically not taught—at home or at school—about the importance of the breath and its impact on the mind and body. . . . Observe how you breathe. There are different patterns that relate to different emotions. Just as your mind influences the breath, you can influence the state of your mind through the breath as well."[33]

Research supports Sri Sri's observations. A revealing study[34] by Belgian psychologist Pierre Philippot shows that your emotions change your breathing. In Philippot's study, his colleagues measured people's breathing patterns when the participants felt emotions like sadness, fear, anger, and happiness. The research team found that each emotion was associated with a distinct way of breathing.

When we experience anxiety, for example, we are likely to take rapid, shallow breaths. When we feel calm, we take deep, slow breaths. Laughter and sobbing are other examples of how the breath accompanies emotional states. When we come home from a long, exhausting day, we slump down onto the sofa and . . . sigh.

More interesting and revealing than Philippot's initial study was his follow-up study.[35] The researchers invited a different group of participants to breathe in the patterns that corresponded to the various emotions from the first study. Then they asked the participants how they felt. Lo and behold, the participants started to feel the emotions that corresponded to the breathing patterns! In other words, when they took deep, slow breaths, the participants felt calm, and when they took rapid shallow breaths, they felt anxious or angry.

The finding that we can change how we feel by using our breath is revolutionary. Given that it is so difficult to change our emotions using thoughts—for instance, "talking yourself out of" intense anger or anxiety—learning to use the breath is a powerful and liberating tool for handling stress so we can perform at our best. One study found that just by giving participants the simple instruction to slow down their breath, researchers were able to reduce the anxiety felt by participants in a stressful decision-making situation.[36]

In a study I ran[37] using a breathing intervention for veterans returning from Iraq and Afghanistan who were dealing with trauma, we found that the breathing practices significantly restored their resilience. I researched the benefits of Sri Sri Ravi Shankar's breathing technique (the *Sudarshan Kriya*) because I had heard of its benefits for stress and trauma.[38] When they came into the study, many of the veteran participants suffered from acute anxiety and post-traumatic stress. After immersing themselves in an intensive weeklong breathing program,[39] however, their symptoms decreased significantly. They were able to relax, and the results were maintained one month and one year out, suggesting permanent improvement.

Breathing is a tool that we have on hand all the time to help us in stressful situations, such as being stuck in traffic on the way to work. Below is an example of how breathing helped someone in arguably the most stressful type of commute there is: a military convoy in a war zone.

The experience of Jake Dobberke, a twenty-six-year-old Marine Corps officer from Iowa, exemplifies the power of breathing to calm the mind. The war in Afghanistan was raging, and Jake was the officer in charge of the last vehicle in his convoy. The vehicle in question is called an MRAP—which stands for Mine Resistant Armor Protected vehicle. As the convoy drove along, Jake's MRAP rolled over an improvised explosive device. There was an extremely loud blast, and despite its armor, the MRAP was damaged. As the vehicle came to a halt and the dust settled, Jake looked down and saw that his legs were severely fractured. He could see muscle and bone exposed where his pants were torn.

In this incredibly traumatic moment, Jake remembered a breathing technique he had learned. He had read a book for active service members (*On Combat* by Lieutenant Colonel Dave Grossman) that described "tactical breathing." This exercise involves breathing in and out in a pattern of four-second counts and breath holds as a way to calm the adrenaline rush and fight-or-flight response. Remembering to breathe in this manner, Jake was able to keep his cool, to check on the well-being of his Marines, to ask his driver to send out a signal for help, to prop up his legs, to tourniquet them, and when all his responsibilities were met and he had ensured everyone's safety, to lie down and rest as he waited for help to arrive. It was only then that he lost consciousness.

"I was doing the breathing because I thought otherwise I was going to go into shock," Jake explained. "Later on, I found out that given the amount of blood I was losing, if I had not had the calmness and presence of mind to tie the tourniquets, I would have bled out and died or fallen into a coma." I saw Jake about a year after he returned from Afghanistan. The lower half of his legs had had to be amputated. Although he says it hurts to even stand in his prosthetics, I was moved to see him get up and join his friends on the dance floor at my wedding.

According to Stephen Porges, professor at the University of North Carolina and distinguished university scientist at Indiana University Bloomington, one reason slow breathing has an immediate effect is that it activates the vagus nerve—the tenth cranial nerve, which is linked to our heart, lungs, and digestive system—and thus slows down the sympathetic (fight-or-flight) and adrenal systems.[40] In so doing, it rapidly calms us down. And with a calm mind, we handle situations more effectively. Porges explains that abdominal breathing—using the diaphragm—is particularly beneficial, as are lengthened exhales. Exhales slow the heart rate; the longer we spend on the outbreath, the more our nervous system relaxes. In this way, exhales activate our parasympathetic (rest-and-digest) system, coaxing greater relaxation into our bodies and minds and helping us feel more peaceful. By controlling your breathing, you can use a voluntary mechanical behavior to make a profound change on your state of mind.[41]

So what does this mean for us? We can use our breath whenever we experience a stressful event. It is an incredible tool that is accessible to you anytime and anywhere—whether it is an interview you are nervous about, an interaction that is upsetting, or a big public talk.

BREATH TRAINING TO BUILD RESILIENCE

While voluntarily changing your breath can help you calm down in a particular situation, the long-term effects of a daily breathing practice—just like those of a daily exercise routine—are even more pronounced.

Preliminary studies have found that regularly practicing breathing exercises normalizes your level of cortisol—the "stress hormone."[42] As a regular practice, breathing can recondition your body to a state of greater calm, helping it bounce back from stress more quickly and perhaps reducing reactivity in the face of challenges. Similarly to a marathon runner who trains her body regularly as a prelude to running longer stretches, you can use daily breathing exercises to prepare your nervous system to be resilient in the face of stressful events, like a big meeting, interview, or first date, so that you perform at your best and recover more quickly thereafter.

Breathing exercises may also naturally increase energy. On average, we only use 10–30 percent of our lung capacity. In other words, we are not performing at our peak energy level. Athletes, in contrast, have learned to use up to 100 percent of their lung capacity to improve endurance and stamina. While the resilience of adults' nervous systems usually decreases with age, this decline is less rapid in professional athletes[43] and others who engage in intense cardiovascular activity—because they generally breathe slower. Yet another reason why cardiovascular exercise is a great stress reliever.

It may seem paradoxical that breathing both decreases stress and increases energy. In our overcommitted, overstressed culture, we don't usually associate high energy with calm. And that misunderstanding explains why we feel we need stress to get things done.

A University of Wisconsin–Madison student who participated in a breathing workshop I conducted told me that since learning breathing and meditation, he was feeling so calm and blissful that he was seriously concerned he would "lose his edge." He worked with the US Marshals and was understandably worried that he would lose his alertness because he was so relaxed—with potentially life-and-death consequences.

Because of the widely held notion that stress is essential to success, it's natural to worry that being relaxed and letting go of tension might affect performance. However, having a calmer state of mind—rather than a stressed one—will help us respond to any situation more rationally and thoughtfully. When we are stressed, we often make rash and impulsive decisions, react too quickly, and say or do things we may later regret. Moreover, our sympathetic (fight-or-flight) nervous system does not shut off and we exhaust ourselves rapidly.

If you strengthen your resilience, you will still be able to respond effectively to life's challenges and experience enough "good" stress to perform at your best as circumstances require—but without paying the cost.

Finally, breathing exercises allow your sympathetic nervous system to rest when it is not needed. They help you relax faster and sleep better after you get home from work. Because you unwind fully during rest periods, you recover your body's natural resilience and are able to meet life's challenges with poise. It allows you to function at peak energy yet without the physical and psychological costs of anxiety and adrenaline overload.

In other words, being calm *and* energized is not only possible through the breath but it is also the *ideal* state: When you are facing a social, creative, or professional endeavor, being highly alert yet also peaceful helps you think, work, and communicate more clearly. You can perform with heightened energy but also come home at the end of the day and relax naturally. The body—unaffected by external stimulants or depressants—is then able to regain its resilience and bounce back from the dozens of small stressful events you experience every day.

PUTTING IT INTO PRACTICE

If you have a fast-paced life, slowing down may seem like a challenge. We're so used to running around and being addicted to the "speed" of life that making this shift to a slower gear seems down right foreign. However, you can learn to tap into your natural resilience. Consciously make time for calming activities. They are vital to your nervous system and well-being. Schedule them into your other top priorities, like taking a shower or brushing your teeth. We usually emphasize habits that make us look and feel good on the outside (grooming ourselves, putting on makeup, showering, and so on), but forget to do the same for what makes us feel good on the inside.

When you slow down, you may experience anxiety because you are so used to operating at a faster pace. This is normal—just go with it. A few years after returning to the United States, Jake Dobberke participated in a breathing workshop for veterans after hearing about my research study. Breathing helped him relax his racing mind, but he also found that as he relaxed, painful memories of his accident resurfaced. By sticking to the breathing program, however, he was able to move past this old trauma and anxiety. "It's been a life-enhancing process that has helped me continue to move forward," he says. Retraining your nervous system doesn't happen in a day, especially if you've been living at high velocity for a while. The good news, however, is that it is possible to retrain your physiology and nervous system. Here are a few ways you can start.

TAKE A BREATH

At first, it may seem silly to do breathing exercises. It may even seem boring. But you'll notice the effects immediately. Here are some strategies to help you get started.

Your breath is with you all the time; it's the most accessible tool you have, and it's invisible. You can practice breathing for well-being no matter where you are, without anyone noticing. At a board meeting that is getting contentious, or when your child is throwing a temper tantrum in the backseat, or when you're exhausted and still have hours of work ahead, take a breather.

The most basic way to develop a relationship with your breath is to take a few minutes, each day, to close your eyes and bring your total attention to your breath. Notice whether it is fast or slow, deep or shallow.

Soon enough, thanks to this practice, you will begin to notice that your breathing shifts with your feelings and emotions during the day. For example, you will naturally take a deep breath during challenging times or find that your breath quickens with anxiety or anger. As you become more aware of your breath, you'll also start to gain more control over it and your feelings in the moment. Thanks to that awareness, when you feel fear coming on, for example, you may notice your breath speeding up and becoming shallower. At that point you can consciously slow it down and breathe into your abdomen to relax. With practice, you will know to take deep and slow belly breaths whenever you encounter a challenging situation.

Here is a simple technique you can practice daily or during difficult situations.

Alternate Nostril Breathing

This gentle yoga-based breathing exercise can help cool the mind and emotions. You may notice that at any given time one nostril is dominant (that is, air flows more smoothly through one nostril and only partially through the other). The dominant nostril alternates throughout the day. One of the reasons this exercise—alternate nostril breathing—may have calming and balancing effects on the mind is that this exercise can unblock both nostrils and allow for greater airflow. To practice, follow these steps:

1. Place the index and middle finger of the right hand between the eyebrows, the thumb on the right nostril, and the ring finger and pinky on the left nostril. The left hand rests on your lap, palm facing up.

2. Take a deep breath in and, closing the right nostril with your thumb, breathe out through the left nostril.

3. Then take a deep breath in through the left nostril, close the left nostril with your ring finger and pinky at the end of the inhale, and exhale through the right nostril.

4. Take a deep breath in through the right nostril and, closing the right nostril with the thumb, exhale on the left side. Then start over.

Do this with your eyes closed for about five minutes. Notice the effects on your body and mind. Yogic breathing practices present little or no risk to a healthy individual, though practitioners may occasionally feel initial tiredness or fatigue, transient tingling sensations, light-headedness, or feelings of euphoria or dysphoria. It is always advisable to work with a trained and certified instructor.

EASE INTO YOUR BODY

Although I highly recommend breathing practices as a daily routine, there are also other ways to balance your nervous system. You probably have your own favorite activities that restore your energy and calm the mind, such as swimming or yoga, walks with your dog in nature, or cuddling with your child. These activities slow down your thoughts and bring ease to your body and nervous system. Here are some examples:

- **Go for a walk.** Studies have shown that a simple walk in nature (as opposed to an urban environment) can significantly decrease anxiety, preserve positive mood, and even improve memory.[44] This benefit is not restricted to country dwellers alone. If you live in a city, choose a park or a tree-lined street. Even just looking at photographs of greenery for 40 seconds can give you a boost and increase your attention levels.[45] Moreover, nature can inspire an experience of awe at the view of a landscape. Research on awe,[46] which is often inspired by beautiful natural sceneries like a starlit sky or a vast horizon, suggests that it slows our perception of time (which is the opposite of what happens with stress) by bringing us into the present moment, and thereby enhances well-being and decreases stress.

- **Take care of your body.** As a result of our distracted lifestyle, we often don't listen to our bodies, or—as we've discussed in this chapter—we try to compensate for the stress we feel with habits that harm our health. We eat the wrong foods, drink, stay up too late, and forget to exercise—or we overexercise. We forget that physical well-being influences mental and emotional well-being. We don't realize that the way we treat our bodies influences our stress levels and determines whether we are able to tap into our natural resilience. As anyone who has started a healthy diet or exercise regimen knows, when we start to take care of the body, we naturally feel better, and with a positive state of mind, our whole outlook on life changes.

- **Engage in slow-paced activities.** If running is your way to relieve stress—as healthy as that is—try also including slower-paced exercise into your schedule. Look for activities that don't involve too much intensity and strain. If you usually go for an intense hot yoga or a power yoga class, instead try yin yoga or restorative yoga or tai chi. Select an activity that is deliberately slow and doesn't involve much effort.

- **Hug a loved one.** Although it often seems that our schedules are too busy for spending time with friends or family, other than a quick catch-up call in the car on the way to work, it's worth it to carve out opportunities to be in the presence of loved ones and share physical affection. One study even showed that hugs are associated with lower stress and stress-related health problems.[47]

Whether you opt for breathing classes or other soothing activities, these practices all build upon themselves. Just like going to the gym, it takes repetition and daily commitment before you see a shift in your nervous system.

Although no one expected António Horta-Osório to return after his ten-week medical leave, he did. Not only did he surprise everyone by returning, but he also continued to turn Lloyds Bank around, and the bank resumed paying dividends to its shareholders for the first time since 2008.[48] Even when chronic stress is wearing us out, we can bounce back.

Athletes put their bodies under stress at each training session and competition, but they are only as successful as the speed at which they recover physiologically. Your daily stresses may be different from those of an athlete, but the concept is the same: your success is determined by the speed of your recovery.

By tapping into your natural resilience through breathing and other calming exercises that activate the rest-and-digest part of your nervous system, you can learn to reduce stress and accomplish more than you ever thought possible.

———

THREE

MANAGE YOUR ENERGY

THE HIDDEN BENEFITS OF CALM

Energy, not time, is the fundamental currency of high performance.
—*Jim Loehr and Tony Schwartz*, The Power of Full Engagement[1]

Moving slowly, then fast, the two opponents wrap their limbs around each other. The only sound in the room is the thump of their bodies as they move around the mat as one. No wonder the practice sessions are referred to as "rolling." In jujitsu, the Brazilian martial art derived from judo, most of the action takes place on the floor. Jujitsu became popular during an Ultimate Fighter Championship tournament—a mixed martial arts event in which, in its original form, competitors would fight any weight class multiple times a day in any style with few rules. Royce Gracie,[2] Brazilian jujitsu legend who first introduced this fighting style to the championships in 1993, is considered one of the most influential fighters in the history of mixed martial arts after winning successive tournaments and defeating men who were much bigger and stronger than himself. Weight is usually an advantage in martial arts. Gracie demonstrated that it doesn't have to matter as long as you have skill.

Mike Heitmann,[3] a police officer who works night shifts in some of the most dangerous areas of Southern California and is a black belt in jujitsu, explained this counterintuitive idea to me. I met Mike when he came to a breathing and meditation class I taught for veterans. (Mike is also a US Marine Corps combat veteran who fought as an infantryman in Fallujah, one of the most deadly battles of the Iraq War.) The deep relaxation he experienced in class prompted him to share the secret to succeeding in jujitsu: energy management.

In a fight, straining and exerting yourself only exhausts you. You lose your cool and make mistakes. You burn out, and your opponent defeats you. By instead remaining calm, you conserve your energy and can intuit the best way to make your next move. To win a jujitsu match, the key is not to fight hard but to let go—not to rev yourself up but to release all strain and stress. Ironically, victory comes when you stop struggling.

All too often in our culture, we believe that, like the traditional fighter who exerts himself in an effort to overcome his opponent with brute force, we can be successful only by straining: we have to give our all every minute of the day, exerting all the intensity we can muster and relying on our iron will to help push us through the work and our fears. But, like the traditional fighter, we often end up exhausted and burned out.

The intensity we pour into our work and lives comes at a high cost: burnout. Psychologists define professional burnout as feeling drained and emotionally exhausted. You may even experience depersonalization (alienation from yourself). As a result, you are not yourself and you are unable to accomplish work to the usual extent.[4] Across professional fields, we are reaching high levels of burnout:

- Human service professionals like teachers, health-care workers, and social workers are especially susceptible to burnout.[5] For example, 45 percent of physicians in the United States are considered burned out.[6]

- Financial professionals also experience high levels of burnout: 50–80 percent of bankers worldwide are completely burned out. In the United States alone, 60 percent of male bankers and 70 percent of female bankers are burned out.[7]

- In the nonprofit sector, 45 percent of young employees insist that their next job will not be in the nonprofit sector, citing burnout as one of the two reasons they won't stay.[8]

Maybe you have felt some signs of it yourself. You are exhausted at the end of the day. You have tense shoulders, a tight jaw; you grind your teeth. Perhaps you have experienced some of the burnout symptoms outlined by the Mayo Clinic:[9]

- becoming cynical or critical at work;

- dragging yourself to work and having a hard time motivating yourself once there;

- becoming irritable or impatient with colleagues or clients;

- lacking the energy needed to be productive;

- lacking satisfaction when you achieve something;

- feeling disillusioned about your work.

Our intensity is not the only reason we experience burnout at work; other factors, such as lack of challenge, variety, or agency, also play a role.[10] However, whereas you cannot always control these other factors, the one thing you do have a say over is how you spend your energy. As Mike explained, when you put all your energy into the fight, you wear yourself out and eventually lose. The person who ends up winning is the one who has remained cool under pressure and saved his energy, deploying it consciously and deliberately when he most needs it.

Calmness, it turns out, is the key to better energy management. Cultivating calmness keeps you happy and helps you consistently achieve your goals, doing your best work without exhaustion.

Let's first look at what we are actually spending our energy on.

THE COST OF INTENSITY

Why are we always exhausted at the end of a workday? Why do we come home wiped out, with barely enough energy to make dinner before collapsing for the night? Normally, when we think about being tired, we think of physical reasons: lack of sleep, intense exercise, or long days of physical labor. Elliot Berkman,[11] professor of psychology at the University of Oregon, points out that in our day and age, when few of us have physically demanding jobs, we are wiping ourselves out through psychological factors. After all, the physical effort we exert in our day jobs does not warrant the fatigue we experience when we get home.

"Does your body get tired until you really can't do anything at all?" asks Berkman. "Actually, it would take a long time to get to that point of complete physical exhaustion." If you are a construction worker, a farmer toiling in a field, or a medical resident working both day and night shifts, then yes, physical exhaustion might be the reason for your fatigue. But otherwise, Berkman points out, your fatigue is mostly psychological. I don't mean that the fatigue "is just in your head" (although, as I'll explain later, to some degree it is). I mean that you feel tired because the following three psychological factors drain you: high-intensity emotions, self-control, and high-intensity negative thoughts.

HIGH-INTENSITY EMOTIONS

Psychologists distinguish emotions along two dimensions: positive–negative on the one hand, and high intensity–low intensity on the other. In other words, is the emotion positive (like *elated, serene*) or negative (like *angry, sad*)? And is it high intensity (like *elated, angry*) or low intensity (like *serene, sad*)?

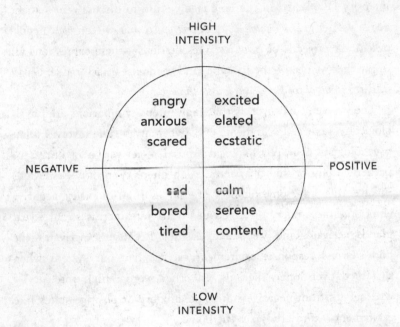

Research shows that we—especially Westerners, and Americans in particular—thrive on *high-intensity* positive emotions. Research by Jeanne Tsai of Stanford University, with whom I conducted several studies, shows that when you ask Americans how they would ideally like to feel, they are more likely to cite high-intensity positive emotions like *elated* and *euphoric* than low-intensity positive emotions like *relaxed* or *content*.[12] In other words, Americans equate happiness with high intensity. East Asian cultures, on the other hand, value *low-intensity* positive emotions like *serenity* and *peacefulness*.

When Jeanne and I ran a study to figure out why Americans value high-intensity positive emotions, we found that Americans believe they need high-intensity emotions to succeed—especially to lead or influence. In a study we ran, for example, people wanted to feel high-intensity positive emotions like excitement when they were in a role that involved leading or trying to influence another person.[13] This intensity is reflected in the language we use to discuss achievement goals: we get *fired up, pumped,* or *amped up* so that we can *bowl* people over, *crush* projects, or *crank out* presentations—these expressions all imply that we need to be in some kind of intense attack mode. *Go get it, knock it out of the park,* and *muscle through.*

The problem, however, is that high-intensity emotions are physiologically taxing. Excitement, even when it is fun, involves what psychologists call "physiological arousal"—activation of our sympathetic (fight-or-flight) system. High-intensity positive emotions involve the same physiological arousal as high-intensity negative emotions like anxiety or anger: our heart rate increases, our sweat glands activate, and we startle easily.[14] Because it activates the body's stress response, excitement can deplete our system when sustained over longer periods. In other words, high intensity—whether it's from negative states like anxiety or positive states like excitement—similarly taxes the body.

High-intensity emotions are also mentally taxing. It's hard to focus when we're physiologically aroused and overstimulated. We know from brain-imaging research that when we're feeling intense emotions, the amygdala is activated. We need to use effort and emotion-regulation strategies from a different part of our brain, located in the prefrontal cortex, to calm ourselves enough to get our work done.[15] And this emotion regulation itself requires effort, as I'll explain later.

The result? You tire easily. Whether you're getting amped up with anxiety or with excitement to finish a project on a deadline, you are draining yourself of your most important resource: energy.

Excitement, of course, can be a positive emotion and it certainly feels a lot better than stress. But just as a sugar high may feel great for a while, it sends your body into a physiological high that can end with a crash. You are bound to feel tired sooner than if you had remained in a calm state.

SELF-CONTROL

Self-control—the discipline to stick to your goals in the face of distractions—is the second way we mismanage energy, thereby unnecessarily fatiguing ourselves. Whether you call it willpower, grit, or self-mastery, it is the mental determination to get the job done despite your feelings, the lure of alternative attractions, and hardships you have to endure. It is critical to success.

"I can resist everything except temptation," said Oscar Wilde.[16] Many of us can identify with his words. It's no surprise that, across fifty countries, people consistently selected "self-control" as the trait they thought they had least of.[17]

We tend to exert the most self-control when we are at work. Think of how strong the temptation is to give your boss or colleagues a piece of your mind when they criticize your efforts, to sleep rather than put extra work into a document due the next morning, or to answer a personal e-mail instead of returning a colleague's call. Our urge to respond to digital distractions in particular is strong. In a classic psychology experiment you have probably heard of, Pavlov noticed that after getting a dog used to being fed whenever a bell rang, the dog started to salivate at the sound of the bell. This reaction—called classical conditioning—is what happens to us when we see a new e-mail pop into our in-box or hear the chime marking the arrival of a new text message. We get a rush. Research shows that we have a natural inclination to shift attention to things that are novel and new.[18] It's far more exciting to check the contents of a brand-new message than to work on the same old daily tasks.

All day long we try—some days more successfully than others—to inhibit these urges and stay on task when we are at work. And this self-control is deeply exhausting. It depletes our energies in four ways:

- Controlling your impulses. Staying on task as opposed to giving up or giving way to distractions (checking Facebook) or temptations (leaving work early to meet friends).

- Controlling your performance. Persisting and giving your best despite having worked an eighty-hour week on little sleep.

- Controlling your behavior (especially your emotional expressions). Maintaining a professional tone and demeanor even when the work atmosphere is hostile and your colleagues or managers make decisions you do not agree with.

- Controlling your thoughts. Focusing on your work despite the many thoughts that pop into your mind. For example, "I'm tired, I want to go home." Or "Maybe I should just quit my job." Or "I wonder if my significant other is upset about what I said." Or fantasizing about your next vacation.

As I touched on in the last chapter, studies[19] by late Harvard psychologist Daniel Wegner suggest that self-control involves a lot of mental effort—and therefore can be taxing. In his theory, coined "ironic processes," he explains that the very act of suppressing a thought (the classic "don't think of a white bear") makes you monitor whether you're successful at suppressing that thought—thereby constantly bringing to mind the unwanted thought! You are basically wrestling with two impulses at once: you are focusing on your goal and what you want to accomplish, but at the same time you are hyper-aware of competing desires, thoughts and impulses. When you apply this phenomenon all day long to your professional life, your social life, your emotional life and your health, is it any wonder we are exhausted by the end of the day?

This fatigue may be the reason why, the more self-control we exert, the more likely we are to lose control. If you've ever started a diet, exercise regimen or New Year's resolution, you know how difficult it can be to keep up. All too often, our efforts fail.

Roy Baumeister, Florida State University professor and world expert on self-control, has demonstrated repeatedly that exerting self-control requires great effort. He compares self-comfort to a muscle, which can strengthen but also wear out with time.[20] After a while, it gets tired and weakens.

In a series of studies looking at a range of scenarios, Baumeister showed that when participants exerted self-control during the first exercise of a study, they were more likely to be impulsive and to lack self-control in the next exercise, showing signs of what appeared to be "self-control fatigue," or as he coined it, *ego depletion*. These studies led Baumeister to argue that self-control is a limited resource. For example, in his classic study,[21] the researchers baked chocolate chip cookies, filling their lab with a delicious aroma. They then brought in the participants. Some participants were invited to eat the chocolate chip cookies and a bowl of chocolates laid out before them. Others were told to eat the radishes that were displayed next to the tempting cookies and chocolates. Then they were given an exercise: working on a puzzle that was, unbeknownst to them, unsolvable. Researchers found that participants who had had to exert self-control by eating radishes instead of the tempting cookies and chocolates more quickly gave up trying to solve the puzzle than those who had eaten the chocolates or a control group that had not been shown the chocolates or radishes.

In another experiment,[22] half the participants were asked to argue in favor of something that they opposed (student tuition raises) whereas the other half did not have to do this part of the exercise. Both sets of participants were then given the unsolvable puzzles to work on. Again, participants who had argued in favor of something they were against gave up working on the puzzles more quickly. Under certain circumstances such as these, exerting self-control, whether in the case of sensory pleasures like eating chocolate or personal beliefs, weakens it.

Despite contradictory evidence since Baumeister first showed this effect, over two hundred studies[23] align with his findings. While this data suggests self-control fatigue may not take place in all circumstances and for everyone (and as I will discuss, there are ways to prevent it[24]), Baumeister's classic findings remain worth considering.

Ever found that your self-control is strong in the morning but then wanes later in the day, maybe even completely diminishing by nighttime? Again, this phenomenon may be due to self-control fatigue. Exerting self-control during the day—for example, controlling your mood at work—may make you have lapses at night, e.g., with regards to alcohol intake.[25] Coping with stress all day may make you more likely to cheat on your diet when you get home.[26] In the morning, you might have the willpower to get out of bed and hit the gym. But after a long day of inhibiting yourself—watching what you say in front of your colleagues, saying no to the burger and fries at lunch in favor of a salad, and resisting the temptation to read some blog posts when you should be responding to work e-mail—you may find it harder to get yourself to work out.

One study even demonstrated that, as the day goes on, we are more likely to engage in behavior we will regret. In the morning, when our self-control is at its highest, we are less likely to act unethically compared to the end of the day.[27] This "morning morality effect," the researchers found, is in part due to decreasing self-control in the afternoon. A similar study[28] found that people are more likely to cheat or act otherwise unethically after having to resist temptation. Perhaps self-control fatigue explains famous examples of people in high-intensity jobs who have shown major self-control failures like politicians and high-level CEOs embroiled in extramarital or financial scandals. Their work demands are unusually intense, requiring great self-control: their behavior has to be impeccable, their words calculated, their attention constant throughout long workdays. Perhaps the intense need for self-control contributes to their lapses and poor decision-making.

Baumeister suggests there may be a physiological reason why self-control diminishes and then backfires: it physically fatigues us. Baumeister has shown that exerting self-control results in a significant drop in blood-sugar levels.[29] We know that the brain relies on glucose for nearly all its activities—and self-control appears to be particularly taxing. In turn, low blood sugar leads to poor self-control. Researchers compared this loss of self-control to what happens after drinking alcohol. Alcohol, by reducing blood sugar, diminishes our ability to exert self-control.[30]

Self-control and discipline are undeniably helpful. However, in some cases and for some people, exerting too much pressure on yourself may contribute to fatigue. You may even succumb to the very thing you want to avoid.

HIGH-INTENSITY NEGATIVE THOUGHTS

High-intensity thoughts are a third factor that depletes our energy. Our thoughts have the capacity to significantly wear us out. I am not just referring to the type of intense thinking you do when you are focused on a complex task—for example, analyzing data, writing a report, or managing the details of a project. The thoughts exhausting you most may not be directly related to your work: a tendency to worry and catastrophize on one hand, and beliefs about what is going to make you tired on the other.

Worry and Catastrophizing

You may not consider worrying a cause for fatigue, yet continuously having thoughts such as "I'm never going to finish on time! What happens if I mess it all up? How will I ever get this done?!" can significantly tax your energy.

Not surprisingly, research shows that worrying is linked to fatigue.[31] Why? Because by worrying, we are imagining and anticipating negative events. As a consequence, our stress levels elevate, and we enter a fight-or-flight state of physiological arousal. Our body believes it is in danger, and our nervous system is highly activated: our heart rate rises, our palms sweat, our body prepares an immune response. The result: we get tired.

It's often not the things on your to-do list that lead to stress. It's your *worry* about getting them done. For example, have you ever had an item on your list for weeks? Every time you think of it, you get anxious because you still haven't gotten to it. You keep making plans to do it, and it's always in the back of your mind. The very thought of it wears you out. Then, one day, you finally work on that task and you have it done in an hour. It wasn't that big a deal, nor was it tiring. But for weeks now, it has been creating tension that has exhausted you.

Worrying can also lead to rumination. For example, if you are treated unfairly by a colleague, when you come home your mind may still be stuck at work, going over the situation and what you'll do about it tomorrow. Not only do these thoughts drain you mentally, but—by disrupting your sleep—they also keep you from resting and recuperating.

Worrying can also lead you to *catastrophize*—a term psychologists use that means having irrational fears that something terrible will happen. You might imagine worst-case scenarios: "If I don't do well, I will lose my job, and then I will be homeless!" Or when you make a small mistake, you might conclude that you are an utter failure. This kind of negative thinking unnecessarily raises stress levels, fatigues us even more, and brings us down.[32] The result: You have drained your energy.

Beliefs About Fatigue

Finally, your beliefs about what tires you significantly contribute to the exhaustion you feel. In fact, Elliot Berkman points to ground-breaking research that shows that fatigue is often determined by your beliefs more than by actual physiological exhaustion. In a revealing study,[33] Stanford psychologist Carol Dweck and colleagues measured whether people believed their willpower was a limited resource by asking participants to select whether they endorsed statements like "After a strenuous mental activity your energy is depleted and you must rest to get it refueled again" (limited-resource theory) and "Your mental stamina fuels itself; even after strenuous mental exertion you can continue doing more of it" (nonlimited-resource theory). They then measured participants' fatigue after they engaged in an energy-depleting task. She noticed that participants' beliefs determined whether their willpower diminished: if they believed their willpower would diminish, it did. In other words, if you believe that a task is fatiguing, it will be. In another study,[34] participants either completed a tiring task or not and were then given false feedback on how fatigued the task had made them. Those who were told that they were more tired performed worse on a subsequent memory task, regardless of whether they had completed the tiring task or not. Your beliefs about whether something is tiring are so powerful that they predict poorer performance.

These case studies show that your energy levels can be dramatically influenced by your mind, in particular your beliefs and thoughts about your work and how tiring it really is. If you go to work expecting to be depleted, you probably will be. I once had a colleague who hated the large events and conferences we routinely organized. He expected them to be exhausting. On event days, he would walk into the office saying, "It's doomsday!" He was inevitably completely drained afterward and would have to take sick days. Other colleagues, on the other hand, looked forward to these large events. They did not show the same depletion effects. If this phenomenon sounds similar to the placebo effect, you are right. Research is uncovering more and more ways in which our minds determine our abilities and well-being—including how tired or refreshed we feel.

When we push ourselves to the limit mentally—by experiencing high-intensity emotions, exerting too much self-control, or falling prey to worries and false beliefs about what makes us tired—we are draining the energy that is critical for us to do good work. When we are then faced with a challenge or critical task, we are too tired and our cognitive abilities are too compromised for us to perform at our best. The good news is that these habits can all be addressed. We can learn to manage our energy. The secret is to stay calm.

CALM: THE KEY TO ENERGY MANAGEMENT

When we are tired for purely physical reasons (for instance, we ran a marathon), the fatigue usually lasts until our bodies have restored themselves. The solution is simple: rest. However, when the reason we are exhausted is psychological, rest doesn't always do the trick. We need to address these psychological factors at the level of the mind. But how? As we saw in chapter 2, it's hard to control thoughts and feelings. Moreover, while research shows that negative thoughts drain our energy,[35] attempting to control these thoughts leads to even more fatigue.[36] This is where calmness comes into play.

During World War II, the British government created posters to boost the morale of the citizens. One poster read, "Keep Calm and Carry On." This poster was meant to be displayed if the Germans invaded the United Kingdom. Recently, the "Keep Calm and Carry On" poster and humorous variations thereof have been popularized on t-shirts, coffee mugs, bags, and Facebook memes. However, there is more than meets the eye to this wise expression created by a British civil servant in the 1940s. Scientific findings suggest that calmness helps you conserve mental energy, allows you to exercise self-control without effort, and reduces the power of negative thoughts by providing perspective.

HOW CALM PRESERVES YOUR ENERGY

In the West, we value high-intensity emotions. In fact, the only time we prefer low-intensity positive emotions like *calm* is as an antidote to stress and worry. We learn relaxation techniques to relieve stage fright; we take a warm bath to unwind after a hard workweek; or we get a massage to help us recover after a particularly stressful work project is over. But we don't usually associate low-intensity emotions like *calm* with success. Calm can even seem counterproductive. We're calm when we're on vacation, at the beach, or on our mat at the end of yoga class. Not—it seems to us—when we're working on a deal, completing a big project on deadline, or teaching a seminar. Calm brings up images of passivity, laziness, lethargy, or ineptitude.

However, being calm does not make you less productive. Nor does it make you passive. Instead, being calm allows you to get your work done while spending less energy than you otherwise would. Because it is a low-intensity emotion, calm doesn't charge up your physiology. Your heart does not beat faster than normal, your palms don't sweat, and your breathing stays regular. Your body is at ease. As a result, instead of using up your energy throughout the day and depleting yourself rapidly, you conserve your energy and deploy it at will.

You may be thinking that you really enjoy the "kick" of deadline-driven anxiety and excitement. It jolts you into action. Stress and excitement are energizers. That's how "energy" drinks got so popular: the caffeine elevates adrenaline, which is typically secreted in response to stress. But as I described earlier, just as we crash a few hours after drinking an energy drink, we also tire quickly after experiencing high-intensity emotional states.

Of course, I'm not suggesting that you should never feel excitement or other high-intensity positive emotions. They bring us joy. But understanding the physiological impact of both positive and negative high-intensity emotions will allow you to deploy emotions more skillfully. Using the "kick" of high-intensity emotions when you see fit is one thing, but doing so all the time is a poor use of energy. Instead, use high-intensity emotions as tools when you need them. There are situations—perhaps in a team meeting you are leading—in which you want to inspire others and be highly enthusiastic and excited. In other situations—like when you are going through e-mail—you might want to avoid getting amped up for such a mundane task.

Using high-intensity emotions selectively and staying calm the rest of the time allows you to conserve energy over the long run.

For example, do you give your all to every task you do? Are you a perfectionist who simply needs to get it all done, done well, and done *now*? Does everything really need to be absolutely perfect, or can certain tasks be done well while others are just fine with a little less attention and effort? While perfectionism is certainly valuable and can push you to do your best, it also has a dark underbelly because it leads to impossibly high standards and worrying that can lead to burnout.[37] Perfectionism in the workplace (as opposed to in sports or education) leads to even greater risks for burnout.[38] Because they have impossibly high standards, perfectionists live in a constant state of high stress. It is no surprise that perfectionism has been linked to suicidal thoughts,[39] anxiety and depression,[40] and poor performance.[41] Staying calm will allow you to look objectively at how you approach work and to manage your energy accordingly. In many cases, *satisficing* is enough. *Satisficing* means accepting that good is good enough.[42] You could spend all your energy on one work project, but understand that you will be exhausted in the face of subsequent responsibilities. I'm not suggesting you do a half-baked job—just that you don't expect perfection on every detail of every project. Some projects may not need the same degree of attention as others. Calmness will give you the perspective you need and will help you determine when good is good enough.

You may think that being calm will prevent you from making the impact you want. However, staying calm does not prevent you from powerfully making your point. For example, I once volunteered to help organize a large speaker event. Thousands of people would be in attendance. Our leader—Tanuja Limaye—personified calmness. A longtime meditator, she was on top of everything and inspired everyone to do a great job, yet she remained completely peaceful. At one point she had to reprimand one of the staff members for making an error. I observed as she raised her voice and appeared frustrated. But somehow I could tell she wasn't. When someone is angry, you usually can feel it. They may get red in the face, and you can practically sense their heart rate accelerating. Tanuja was outwardly stern and clearly communicated her disappointment. The person she reprimanded definitely got her point. Yet when you observed Tanuja closely, you could she that she remained perfectly calm on the inside. As Tanuja stated the facts to the staff member, she communicated in a strong way, yet without bitterness. She wasn't wound up or deeply upset. Two minutes later, she was laughing at a joke with that same staff member. She had moved on. Job done but no energy was wasted.

WHY CALM IS THE KEY TO EFFORTLESS SELF-CONTROL

We exercise self-control countless times during a regular workday (and in the evenings too!), and it's exhausting us. When we experience high-intensity emotions like excitement or stress, we need extra self-control, because physiological arousal adds one more element to control. For example, your heart is pounding with anxiety over a presentation you have to make, and then you have to exert control not only over your words as you deliver your message, but also over your body so that you don't stutter or lose your train of thought.

Calm states are the key to effortless self-control. Staying calm helps you be present with the task in which you are engaged, making it easier to avoid distractions. Paying attention happens naturally without any need for self-control.

We have an intuitive understanding that if we remain calm we will be better able to focus. In a study I ran, we invited two participants into the lab. The first participant was to follow the instructions of the second participant in a puzzle task, so the first participant had to listen carefully as his partner provided guidance. When I asked the first participant in each pair how they would like to feel during the task, they expressed a desire to feel calm.[43] You have no doubt experienced that your thoughts stop racing when you are relaxed and at peace. Research confirms that your attention to the things around you becomes broader, more inclusive, and sharper when you are calm.[44] You are able to take more in.

Another reason why calm leads to effortless self-control is that you conserve energy and thus you are less tired. As Baumeister's research shows, it is *when we are fatigued* and have drained our energy that self-control fails us.

HOW CALM REDUCES THE IMPACT OF YOUR THOUGHTS

When you are calm, you are better able to control your thoughts and feelings. When we were babies, we focused on our internal world, sensing hunger or thirst and feeling sleepy or scared. As we grow up, the internal world becomes increasingly foreign and distant as we prioritized the outside. As adults, we mostly focus on the external world, paying attention to the things that engage our senses: phones ringing, colleagues walking into the office to talk, urgent e-mail messages, computer screens, newspaper articles, and delicious aromas. As adults, often we tune in to our internal awareness—our thoughts and emotions—only when it sounds an alarm or takes us by surprise, as when we experience pleasure ("Wow, that tasted good!") or pain ("Ouch!"). Maybe we suddenly notice a sore back or neck from sitting at the computer for too many hours at a stretch. Or we may realize our thoughts are racing with fear, or we suddenly get flush with anger, choked up with sadness, or weak-kneed with love.

Although we don't pay much attention to it, internal awareness is far more important than most people realize. Given that negative thoughts and beliefs about what makes us tired have such a powerful effect on our energy levels, it is critical that we recognize them when they arise. Internal awareness allows us to observe these beliefs and thoughts—rather than let them run the show.

You have a neural pathway dedicated to internal awareness in your brain.[45] However, when you are physiologically wound up from high-intensity emotions, it may be harder to access this pathway because other parts of your brain are on high alert. Whether you are experiencing a caffeine high, have anxiety jitters, or are on top of the world with excitement, your thoughts are probably going a mile a minute. You are at the mercy of the state of your mind, your words and decisions a direct reflection of the stress in your system. As a result, your thought process is not as clear or rational as it could be, and you are more likely to act impulsively, saying or doing things you might later regret.

If you are calmer, however, it is easier to tap into internal awareness and observe the mind's activity. You can notice when you are starting to get caught up in anxious and frenzied thoughts and can consciously choose not to yield to those thoughts or to fuel them. Instead, you can observe your thoughts as if you were an audience member watching them on a screen. For example, instead of thinking, "I am worried that my boss will say *x, y,* and *z* at my annual review," repeatedly cycling through worst-case scenarios about what your boss could say, you might simply note, "There's a lot of anxiety coming up right now," without adding fuel to the fire. Instead of thinking, "I absolutely have to do a good job when I give my talk or I'll die of embarrassment," you note to yourself, "I am catastrophizing again." When you are calm, you have greater control over your mind; rather than engaging with those kinds of thoughts and feelings, you will choose to not interact with them. You don't resist them—since, as we've learned, resisting thoughts only makes them stronger. You simply accept that they are there *without identifying* with them. Your feelings are not driving you. Instead of being a slave to impulsive thoughts, you consciously decide what you are going to say or do. Instead of the negative and stressful thoughts draining you, you retain your energy.

Eastern cultures have long held that calm is a source of immense strength and power. The Chinese term *wuwei,* or nonaction, is described as the key to life in Taoism and its foundational text, the *Tao Te Ching.* This text advocates for *wei wu wei,* action without action. This sounds like a riddle, but it's a riddle pregnant with wisdom. One way of interpreting this phrase is that calmness is the "inaction" in the "action." You may be in the middle of a critical client meeting or negotiating the deal of a lifetime, but inside you remain peaceful, calm, and grounded. As a consequence, you are more observant, listen better, communicate more skillfully, and make better decisions. Whether you win or lose, whether you succeed or fail, you come out on top. You remain centered and at ease.

When you are calm, you *are* in a place of power. Because your mind is present, you are able to focus naturally. Calmness is a state in which you don't need self-control—because you already are in control.

Why? Because you have volition over the state of your mind. As Sarah Severn,[46] senior director of Systems Innovation, Sustainable Business and Innovation at Nike, shared with me, "you have a choice about how you react to any circumstances around you. I can react with joy, I can react with depression or feeling like a victim, or I can look at this in a more neutral way as a teaching moment. The biggest influence you can have is to listen to your heart and your highest intention rather than letting the mind run rings around you. If you can do that, the ego takes a backseat and you can have a positive influence on others around you." When you are calm, you will not regret the actions you take, because—rather than simply reacting to the world around you—you choose your actions: they are thoughtful and stem from a clear and objective state of mind. You work with ease rather than strain; you are relaxed rather than tense. Most importantly, you have managed your energy and are not burned out.

HOW TO CULTIVATE CALM

There will be days when you find it challenging to calm your mind, especially in emotionally charged situations or under tight deadlines. How do you nurture calmness so it becomes automatic? One of the best ways to do so is through meditation.

Meditation—sometimes referred to as mindfulness—has grown in popularity over the past decade. It has been the subject of news articles, TV segments, and countless books thanks to a growing body of research on its benefits. As a result, many extremely successful individuals—from TV personality Oprah Winfrey, to CEO of Skoll Global Threats Fund Larry Brilliant, to music industry icon Russell Simmons, and to executive chairman of Ford Motor Company, Bill Ford—have adopted meditation and consider it an indispensable practice in their lives, touting its benefits.

One study showed that meditation can actually buffer you against the tiring effects of self-control.[47] The researchers replicated Baumeister's classic experiment: participants completed a task that depleted their self-control, then worked on a second challenging task. If their self-control was drained from the first task, they typically should do worse or give up more easily on the second task. In this study, the difference was that some of the participants meditated between the tasks while others did not. The scientists found that the meditating participants performed as well on the second task as participants who had not completed the first task at all. Meditation therefore appears to be a useful tool to recharge your tank and prevent depletion after challenging tasks requiring self-control. Meditation has also been linked with reduced stress and anxiety, as well as enhanced emotion regulation, further helping us retain energy.[48]

If you've never tried meditation, you might be intimidated. In fact, it's one of the simplest exercises you can do. As a first step, simply close your eyes and turn your attention inward. In other words, rather than focusing on the world around you—the sounds, sights, smells, and so on—focus on what is happening inside your body and mind. It doesn't have to get more complicated than that. The simple act of looking inward for just a few minutes can be quite restorative. Start with five minutes at a time. Become aware of physical sensations first:

any physical feelings in your body, the movement of your breath, your heart rate, the feel of the floor or your chair below you, the clothes on your body, and any jewelry or rings you are wearing. Then move your awareness to thoughts and feelings: notice them without engaging with them, as if they were on a movie screen. Gradually increase your meditation time as you grow in confidence. An even simpler way to meditate is to focus on the breath, one breath at a time. This exercise can seem maddeningly boring, but you will find that, over time, the result is a much calmer state of mind. There are lots of meditation classes, books, and CDs that offer guidance on how to meditate and that propose different techniques that might appeal to you. There are also a number of apps on the market, such as Sattva or Headspace, that offer meditations for beginners.

If you are not ready for meditation, then simply choose a physical posture that invites calm. As we saw in chapter 2, changing your physiology can dramatically change how you feel. A fascinating field of research called *embodied cognition* has demonstrated that just changing our bodily posture can shift our state of mind. There is real wisdom in the expression "you might want to sit down" before hearing alarming news, or advice to "sleep on" a difficult problem. Let's say, for example, that you are wound up with anxiety or anger about something and can't figure out how to calm down. A brain-imaging study out of Texas A&M showed that the simple act of lying down can reduce feelings of anger and hostility.[49] Exercise and the breathing exercises described in chapter 2 are other obvious ways of changing your physiology to calm your body and mind. You might also consider going to a gentle, awareness-based yoga or tai chi class or even a stretching class.

Make these practices part of your daily routine until internal awareness and calmness become second nature. Research studies suggest that the benefits of meditation-like practices build over time in cumulative fashion. The more you meditate, the more you reap the benefits,[50] so that a state of calm starts to rule your day.

HOW TO RESTORE YOUR MENTAL ENERGY

Remaining calm will help you manage your energy so that it does not drain as quickly. However, there will be times when you *are* drained and need to restore mental energy levels. Managing mental energy means knowing when you need to replenish yourself (without caffeine or high-intensity emotions). Here are some empirically validated ways to restore energy when it is depleted.

DO SOMETHING THAT MAKES YOU FEEL POSITIVE

In one study,[51] participants who were shown a funny film clip or were given a surprise gift did not display fatigue after exerting self-control. Another[52] demonstrated that, for religious individuals, prayer helped buffer against depletion. Research aside, you know best the kinds of activities that you find uplifting. Create a list and keep it handy, so you don't have to figure out what to do when you feel mentally exhausted. For example, if you're at work, replenishing your energy might mean going for a walk, taking a break, watching a funny YouTube video, looking at pictures of your loved ones, meditating, or engaging in a random act of kindness for a colleague.

TURN WHAT YOU'RE DOING INTO SOMETHING YOU WANT TO BE DOING

There are lots of activities that involve effort but don't tire you. Why? Because you love them! Elliot Berkman reminds us, "If you feel tired but something really fun comes along, you all of a sudden have a second wind." Berkman, who admits to having a sweet tooth, told me that sometimes he gets home after a long day feeling exhausted and craving ice cream. If there is no ice cream in the freezer, he still is able to muster the energy to go buy it—even when it involves putting on a winter jacket and snow boots, shoveling the driveway, and warming up the car to drive to a store that is twenty minutes away. People have plenty of energy for the things they want to do.

There is truth to this saying, attributed to Confucius: "Choose a job you love and you will never have to work a day in your life." Now, the problem is that we can't always choose to do what we love—either in our careers or in our personal lives. However, we *can* choose how we approach our work so we can enjoy it more. Rather than thinking of work as work, reframe it by thinking of what you love about it. Sound easier said than done? Here are a few research-backed suggestions.

Remember the Big Picture

Focus on the *why* rather than the *how* of a task or job. For example, if you are working on a dissertation or launching a start-up and you have lost your motivation and energy, remember why you are doing it: you are completing a dissertation because you are passionately interested in the topic and look forward to becoming a professor and teaching about it; your start-up will revolutionize your field and completely change the way people do things.

Understanding how your work connects to what you care about and to your values will restore your energy. For example, if your company sells a certain device or product and you value making a difference in people's lives, you can think about how that device or product is helping people to fulfill their needs. Organizational psychologist Adam Grant, professor of management at the Wharton School of Business, has researched this effect.[53] Grant studied a university call center in which employees made calls to raise money for financial aid. After Grant brought in one of the student recipients to explain what a big difference the aid had made in his life, there was a steep increase in productivity at the center. Why? Because the center workers were personally moved when they saw the impact their work was having. Their work became a mission with a purpose.

What happens if you are toiling away at a desk job that you don't particularly like and that is not related to your passions for hiking and your family? In that case, think about how it is indirectly related to your passions. For example, you may be working long hours and taking on extra shifts because it provides income for your next trip to the Sierras. Or your job may be funding your child's college tuition account or a big end-of-year family vacation. Remembering how your job allows you to indulge your passions will help you refocus on the big picture. You will go back to appreciating the job rather than experiencing it as a burden.

When you focus on the big picture, you remember why you care about this work. As a consequence, you start to *want* to do what you are doing rather than thinking you *have* to do it. It's the difference between what psychologists call *intrinsic* motivation (being motivated from within—for example, because you know it will make a difference or because you love doing it) and *extrinsic* motivation (being motivated by an external reason, like a boss who is breathing down your neck or the need to bring home a paycheck).[54] Research has shown that when people are motivated from within, because they love what they do (for instance, a basketball player who loves playing basketball), they do it without being told or pressured. It becomes a privilege and a joy to go to work.

When you remember why you *want* to be doing your job, you won't need self-control to do it. In other words, you won't need to expend energy, because you are not exerting self-control.

Practice Gratitude

Research[55] has shown that feeling grateful helps you replenish your energy in the face of fatiguing tasks. Let's say you don't like your job. Regardless, there are always things that warrant being grateful: You have a job when many others don't. Maybe you enjoy some of your colleagues. Maybe there are perks and benefits. Berkman points out that the reason gratitude has such a replenishing effect is that feeling grateful both increases positive emotion and helps you see the big picture.

Detach from Work When You're Not Working

Many people take work home with them at night or do it during their time off. As a consequence, the stress of the day blends into evenings and vacations and eats up recovery time. Sabine Sonnentag, professor at the University of Mannheim in Germany, has found that people who do not know how to detach from work during their off time experience increased exhaustion over the course of one year and are less resilient in the face of stressful work conditions.[56]

Sherron Lumley[57] is a television news producer covering the White House, Capitol Hill, and breaking news for an international audience of 40 million. Although her professional life is based in Washington, DC, Lumley chooses to live in Oregon. During breaking news events in DC, her job is intense. However, when she returns home to Oregon, she remains intentionally out of reach, enjoying her family, hiking in the mountains, canoeing, or restoring her Victorian home. She doesn't check messages until she is at the airport, just before returning to the East Coast. "The time I spend at home recharges me and reminds me of who I am," Lumley told me. "When I return to Washington, I'm able to handle the pressure and pace gracefully, bringing out the best in the news team."

Because she has found that psychological detachment from work is particularly difficult when the job's workload and time pressure are high,[58] Sabine Sonnentag stresses how critical it is to learn to consciously detach from work when it is highly demanding. Sonnentag has found that psychological distance from work is the fastest path to recovery and leads—surprisingly perhaps—to increased productivity. "From our research, one can conclude that it is good to schedule time for recovery and to use this time in an optimal way." Activities that Sonnentag's research confirms help with detachment are exercise,[59] walks in nature,[60] and total absorption in a non-work-related hobby.[61] Positively reflecting about your job after work hours can also help replenish you.

In our busy and overwhelmed culture, we are often urged to manage time better. Time management apps, blogs, and workshops abound. We believe that if only we could manage our time, we would get more done and be happier. However, there are only so many hours in a day, no matter how neatly scheduled you are. A better focus—and one that few people understand—is energy management.

How are you using the energy you have each day? Most people burn it unnecessarily on high-intensity emotions, self-control, and counterproductive thinking. The best way to manage energy is by cultivating calm. The result? Less stress, a clearer mind, and sharper focus to get your work done. You get the same amount of work done, but you remain balanced and enjoy the process. Because you are able to think more clearly, you do a far better job. The best part, of course, is that because you are not as tired, your energy levels remain high. As a result, you are happier and more successful.

FOUR

GET MORE DONE BY DOING MORE OF NOTHING

THE SECRET TO ACCESSING CREATIVITY

Don't underestimate the value of Doing Nothing, of just going along, listening to all the things you can't hear, and not bothering.

—*Pooh Bear in* Pooh's Little Instruction Book

When he received the phone call notifying him that he had been selected to receive the Nobel Prize in Economics, Myron Scholes,[1] professor emeritus at Stanford Graduate School of Business, was not holed up in his office working out equations or reading research papers. He was preparing for a day of golf after giving a breakfast talk.

Many describe Scholes as nothing short of a genius. He is famous for developing innovative and groundbreaking theories in economics, including the Black-Scholes Options Pricing Technology, which helped create the derivatives market and for which he was awarded the Nobel Prize in 1997. But when you ask him how he comes up with his novel insights, he attributes his creativity to time spent *not* working, such as during his daily meditations and walks. Scholes defies the stereotypical image of an academic deeply yet narrowly immersed in one field of study. He reads widely outside of his field and is always ready to discuss his latest favorite book. He is vivacious, curious, and insightful. Belying his age, he is youthful and lively. I always leave our conversations lighter and more inspired.

How does Scholes do it? How is he so productive, insightful, and joyful all at once?

We think successful people are those who are so completely dedicated to their fields that they focus exclusively on their field of expertise: They try to stay on top of every book, article, blog post, or research study published in their area. They think about their work constantly. They approach their work with intense concentration and attention, carefully crossing every *t* and dotting every *i* when they have a problem or issue they need to resolve. In short, they are *focused*.

It's easy to see why most of us buy into the myth that single-minded attention is essential to success. After all, concentration—the ability to get completely absorbed in a task, approaching it with laser-sharp attention—is valued from grade school ("Pay attention! Don't daydream!") through work life. Our ability to stay focused on the task at hand is not only prized and rewarded but absolutely required to get ahead and do well, or so we are told.

Malcolm Gladwell, author of the bestselling book *Outliers,* popularized the idea that anyone can achieve mastery in a skill or art if they put in ten thousand hours of focused practice. Although the research behind this idea has since been called into question,[2] it has nonetheless taken hold of the popular imagination. Why? Because it fits neatly with our theory that all we need to achieve greatness is single-minded focused attention. Practice makes perfect—right?

Focus and concentration are, of course, undeniably important: the better you focus, the faster you absorb information—whether you are learning a technical skill like a musical instrument or computer software program, or an intellectual skill like how to succinctly synthesize concepts from multiple articles.

We believe that the opposite of focus—daydreaming, goofing off, spacing out—is to be avoided. Worse yet, having problems focusing is seen as an obstacle to overcome and even as pathological. We complain about having short attention spans. Newspapers ceaselessly report on attention deficit hyperactivity disorder. Self-help books and productivity bloggers strive to keep us on task with advice and hacks. When we fail to come up with the results we were hoping for, we wonder whether we just aren't working or concentrating hard enough. If we could only stay focused for hours on end as we work on this or that project, report, or presentation, then we could get so much more done.

We've come to consider focus and being *on* as "good," and idleness—especially if it goes on for too long—as "bad" and unproductive. We feel guilty if we spend too much time doing nothing. The saying "Idle hands are the devil's workshop" betrays our belief that having nothing to do inevitably leads to all sorts of bad things. The concept that idleness is bad is so deeply ingrained that many people (84 percent of executives, for example!) cancel vacations to work.[3]

In thinking this way, we make a fundamental mistake. Truly successful people like Scholes don't come up with great ideas through focus alone. They are successful because they make time to *not concentrate* and engage in a broad array of activities like playing golf. As a consequence, they think inventively and are profoundly creative: they develop innovative solutions to problems and connect dots in brilliant ways.

Dwight Eisenhower logged more hours on the golf course than any other US president yet is also regarded as one of the best presidents the United States has ever had.[4] He had a rule on the golf course: Except in the case of emergency, there was to be no talk of politics. Explaining his reasons to a potential presidential candidate, he said:

"Young man, let me tell you something. You are going to work 14 hours a day, seven days a week for the government, and you are going to think you are doing your job. Here is what I want you to know. If that's what you do, there is no way you'll be able to do your job."[5]

THE POWER OF CREATIVITY

According to a 2010 IBM survey[6] of more than 1,500 CEOs spanning sixty countries and thirty-three industries, CEOs believe that *the* most important skill needed to navigate today's complex business world is creativity. The CEOs ranked creativity even higher than rigor, management, discipline, vision, and even integrity. Whether you are a flight attendant juggling family life with travel, a computer engineer developing a new app, or a mom trying to get her children to eat vegetables, creativity is at the heart of what makes you successful. Creativity helps you find better ways to complete your work and come up with novel ideas that make you better at what you do.

Some of the most inventive people in our society have claimed that their game-changing insights arose out of daydreaming or irrelevant and mindless tasks. In 1881, famed inventor Nikola Tesla had fallen seriously ill on a trip to Budapest. There, a college friend, Anthony Szigeti, took him on walks to help him recover. As they were watching the sunset on one of these walks, Tesla suddenly had the insight (rotating magnetic fields) that would lead to the development of modern day's alternating current electrical mechanism.[7]

Similarly, Friedrich August Kekulé, one of the most renowned organic chemists in nineteenth-century Europe, discovered the ring-shaped structure of the organic chemical compound benzene in a daydream of the famous circular symbol of a snake eating its own tail. Composer Ludwig van Beethoven famously said that music just came to him: "Tones sound and roar and storm about me until I have set them down in notes." Even Albert Einstein attributed insight to something beyond linear thinking and logic alone. He turned to music—Mozart in particular—when he was grappling with complex problems and needed inspiration.[8] He is quoted as saying, "All great achievements of science must start from intuitive knowledge. I believe in intuition and inspiration. . . . Imagination is more important than knowledge."[9]

More recently, Woody Allen credits taking showers with helping him "unblock ideas."[10] And in her TED talk, Elizabeth Gilbert, author of the bestseller *Eat Pray Love,* describes the apparent muse or creative genius that seems to alight unexpectedly upon writers, songwriters, and poets when they are in the midst of doing something unrelated to their art.[11]

In a time and age when everyone is overscheduled and overfocused, creativity is more and more prized—it's the key to your effectiveness and success, in life and in business, and it can be a never-ending source of joy and happiness.

HOW DOING NOTHING LEADS TO CREATIVITY

Research shows that there are two main modes of thought—intense focus on the present to achieve current goals, and downtime when we can daydream, let our minds wander, and come up with new ideas. While we give a lot of attention to the former, the latter is actually the secret to creativity.

In chapter 1, I discussed the importance of being present with what you are doing and of not mind-wandering *during* an activity such as work or interactions with other people. In this chapter, however, I discuss the importance of a different kind of mind-wandering: *purposeful* mind-wandering—that is, choosing to take idle time to let your mind unfocus.

Scott Barry Kaufman,[12] scientific director of the Imagination Institute at the University of Pennsylvania and author of *Ungifted and Wired to Create*, explains that being idle and letting your mind wander constitute the optimum state for inventive thought and new perspectives.

Kaufman points out that the two kinds of thinking—linear and creative—align with different neural networks in the brain. The first involves conscious focus on an activity, while the second (sometimes called the default network because it is activated when we are just relaxing) involves thoughts, fantasies, daydreams, and memories that arise when we aren't focused on a particular task. According to Kaufman, we don't want one of these neural systems to be overactive at the expense of the other. Ideally, we would have the ability to switch flexibly from one to the other according to circumstances.

Other studies confirm this idea. Research[13] by University of California Santa Barbara's Jonathan Schooler and colleagues found that you are more creative after you have been daydreaming or letting your mind wander. Their study showed that when people learn a challenging task, they do better if they work first on an easy task that promotes mind-wandering and then go back to the challenging task. Here again, the idea is to balance both kinds of activities (idleness and focus) and to switch between the two to get optimum output.

We need a balance of both focus and rest, because if our minds are constantly processing information, perhaps because of our nonstop schedule and the demands placed upon us by technology, we never get a chance to let our thoughts roam and our imagination drift. If we don't give our minds a break, they cannot engage in the kind of idle activity that leads to creative inspiration.

A study[14] by Marieke Wieth and Rose Zacks confirms that rest is critical for creative thinking. The researchers found that morning people are most creative in the evening, whereas night owls have their biggest breakthroughs in the morning. It might sound counterintuitive, but it also makes sense. The mind can finally drift when the brain goes into a sleepy, relaxed alpha-wave mode.

Salvador Dalí famously engaged in "sleep with a key," in which he would let himself doze off with a key between his fingers and a metal plate below it. When he fell asleep, the key would fall to the ground with a clang, waking him up. He believed that those moments between wake and sleep—a state called *hypnagogia*—kindled his creativity.[15]

These studies suggest that we become more imaginative and visionary by taking time out for ourselves: engaging in purposeless or idle pastimes, giving ourselves the space to be quiet and still, and finding time to have some fun. These three activities help us engage in relaxed mind-wandering with no immediate "to-do" to worry about. You may be doing something that doesn't demand a lot of intellectual resources, such as taking a walk, stamping envelopes, or even doing the dishes, but in fact you are creating inner stillness and room to think. As a result, the insights you need may percolate through.

"The greatest creative ideas don't come from obsessive seven-days-a-week constant focus on a problem," shared Kaufman. "Managers and employees need to understand that creative insights are not going to come from such conscious deliberation. They come from *integration* with more free-floating ideas and emotions that arise during leisure time, daydreaming, recollection of memories, and other connections to your own internal world."[16]

WHY YOUR CREATIVITY IS MIA

For many, the state of idleness described by Kaufman can be difficult to access. While we *all* have creative potential we can access, most of us have simply forgotten how to access it because our education and hectic lifestyle overemphasize linear thinking.

HOW EDUCATION BURIES NATURAL CREATIVITY

Children are undoubtedly the most creative people in our society. They turn living rooms into fortresses, involve stuffed animals in elaborate plots involving heroes and villains, and talk to imaginary friends. Children can turn any situation—whether they are sitting in a waiting room or walking to school—into an opportunity for daydreaming and play. Games emerge out of whatever tools or things they have at their disposal—a running river, a stick or object, a pen, a paper doll, or a bouncy ball. In fact, kids have come up with inventions as diverse as popsicles, trampolines, and earmuffs.[17]

Children's thoughts and ideas flow freely, unrestricted by the demands adults place upon themselves. For example, while waiting at the bus, they might pretend that sticks they find are swords, imagine kingdoms in piles of leaves, or see animals in cloud shapes, while we adults check e-mail, rework our to-do list, send a text, replay an incident that happened at work, or plan the upcoming day. As Pablo Picasso famously said, "All children are artists. The problem is staying an artist when he grows up."[18] If we all have the ability to be creative masters as children, our creative genius must be innate. So where did it go? Our education buried it.

We lose touch with our unbounded childlike mind because both education and professional training impose boundaries, discipline, and rigor on our thinking. Our minds learn to operate in a linear fashion and to reason logically—great skills, of course, but skills that curb creativity when they are overemphasized at the cost of imagination and inventiveness.

Research on divergent thinking—a fancy academic term for creativity—highlights the impact of education on our creativity. *Di-*

vergent thinking refers to the ability to come up with diverse solutions to a problem. It is basically stream-of-consciousness brainstorming. Some of the solutions you come up with may not help solve your problem, but unexpected ideas and connections between concepts emerge that can inadvertently lead to an innovative solution. Convergent thinking, on the other hand, is the process of coming up with a solution through logical and linear reasoning—through what is already known.

What do we learn in school? Convergent thinking. George Land, author of *Grow or Die,* suggests that this kind of training dramatically reduces our natural creativity. He studied a group of 1,600 children at several points in their youth using a test of divergent thinking that he had developed for NASA. He found that between three and five years of age, 98 percent of the children ranked as "divergent thinking geniuses." Between eight and ten years of age, that number had dropped to 32 percent. Between the ages of fifteen and eighteen, the number had dropped down to 10 percent. When Land tested a group of twenty thousand twenty-five-year-olds, he found that only 2 percent could think divergently. Land concludes that while creativity is naturally present at a young age, we unlearn it through our education system.[19]

While Land's study has not yet been published, other peer-reviewed published studies using different creativity tests are arriving at similar results. In July 2010, Dr. Kyung-Hee Kim, a professor at the College of William and Mary, prompted an international dialogue on the "Creativity Crisis" and the importance of creativity in education and business when she published some alarming statistics showing a decline in creativity in today's youth. She found that creativity remained static or declined after the sixth grade and that since 1990 there has been a steady decline in creativity scores while IQ scores have risen.[20] Kim concludes that "people in general are becoming less able to think creatively, and they are less tolerant of creativity and creative people. Especially, younger children are less able to think creatively."

Interestingly, Kim found that there is a negligible correlation between creativity and IQ tests.[21] In other words, even if we hone the skills that help us score high on an IQ test—the linear thinking skills we are taught in school, such as memory and reasoning—those skills do not necessarily mean we will be able to come up with groundbreaking inventions. Of course, linear thinking is certainly a skill everyone needs, but it should not be honed to the exclusion of creativity, which is also essential for success.

NO TIME FOR NONLINEAR THINKING

In addition to schools and workplaces, which value linear thinking alone, we live our lives with so little room for nonlinear thought that even when idle moments present opportunities for creativity, we fail to take advantage of them.

When we are not focused on the "important" stuff, like the requirements of career and family, our attention is in constant demand. We are overstimulated—often by a constant bombardment of technology, which places a heavy burden on our attention. As a consequence, many people spend every waking moment *focused*. Everyone around us—our supervisor at work or our friends and family—expects us to be available all the time through our electronic devices. Interruptions from the various devices we use (text alerts, cell phone calls, and chats) impede idle contemplation.

Even worse, our minds have become trained to constantly check our devices and in-boxes. This habit has become so insidious that we even interrupt ourselves. You may notice that you automatically switch windows to check your e-mail every so often, and the same goes with your phone. Nonlinear thinking requires some level of mind-wandering and rêverie, but our internal "alerts" to check our e-mail and phone needlessly end up short-circuiting this process. Whereas in the past we might have daydreamed while commuting to work on public transportation or standing in line at the grocery store, now we compulsively check e-mail "just in case" or browse Facebook for no good reason. As a consequence, we keep ourselves focused every moment of the day.

Moreover, our days are packed to the brim. Our to-do lists are longer than ever, and our schedules are tightly filled with work meetings and nonwork activities—from going to the gym to volunteering, to book clubs, to picking up the kids from daycare. We try to squeeze productivity out of every hour of the day, not wanting to "lose" any precious time and trying to stay on top of our to-do lists.

Even when schedules and work and social demands leave room for idle time conducive to nonlinear thinking, the concept of idle time has become so foreign that we get bored or uncomfortable whenever we are faced with it. We get anxious or antsy when we "have nothing to do." So we turn right back to our devices and technology or entertainment like television or online videos to occupy that idle time rather than spend time reflecting, relaxing, or engaging in daydreaming. Whether we are standing in line at an airport or in a waiting room at the doctor's office, our tendency is to flip through a magazine, watch the pervasive TV screens, talk or text on the phone, or browse the Internet on our devices.

Professor Timothy Wilson at the University of Virginia began noticing people's discomfort with being by themselves and decided to run several studies in 2014[22] to test how people feel about being alone with their thoughts. He gave participants the option of spending six to fifteen minutes alone with their thoughts or doing a mundane and boring task. He found that, overwhelmingly, people preferred the mundane task to being alone with their thoughts.

Most tellingly, in one study, he gave participants the option of self-administering electric shocks—if they wished—during the thinking portion of the experiment. The researchers found that a large number of people—even those who rated the shock as very unpleasant and said they would pay money not to feel it again—preferred giving themselves electric shocks to sitting in a room alone with their thoughts! In short, the researchers concluded that "most people seem to prefer to be doing something rather than nothing, even if that something is negative."

In an effort to maximize productivity by staying focused and occupied throughout the day, we've left no room for the one thing that can help us succeed and truly be productive: nonlinear thinking and creativity.

Geniuses, on the other hand, know that insights and inventions depend on a wandering mind unconstrained by logic. The creative process requires an openness of mind not confined by rigidity, boundaries, rules, or other mental constraints. So while we believe that success stems from staying focused and being productive nonstop without a minute wasted, the truth is that success depends in large part on unfocusing, relaxing rather than working, and finding time to do nothing—opening up the space in our lives that our brains need for creative processes.

How can we do that?

THE THREE PATHS TO CREATIVE IDLENESS

Purposely letting the mind drift into idleness is a big challenge for most of us because even when we have free time, our minds have a hard time shutting off thoughts about work, worries, and so on. Some people fear that embracing idleness will make them lazy. Or they feel it may get in the way of "getting things done." We are so used to linear thinking that, given time alone, we might draw up a to-do list, a grocery list, or some other plan. Despite the ease with which we accessed it as a child, reaching a state of mind that is not caught up in constant "productive" activity can be challenging as an adult. We have to, in essence, relearn how to be idle.

Practically speaking, there are three ways to access our potential for creativity: learning to unfocus through diversification, making time for stillness and silence, and inviting fun back into our lives.

UNFOCUS THROUGH DIVERSIFICATION

Experts suggest that the key to being idle or to unfocusing is to diversify our activities rather than being constantly focused on a single task. To get a new perspective on something, we actually need to disengage from it. We can diversify in two ways: through mindless tasks or through a broader set of experiences.

Diversifying with Mindless Tasks

Kaufman recommends breaking up time spent assimilating information and working on a task by inserting fifteen-minute periods of more mindless and less focused activity: taking a shower or going for a quick walk (without concentrating on your cell phone) or doing some stretching. "By taking that fifteen-minute period for mindlessness or daydreaming, your attention has been broadened and your mind is now able to make more creative connections between ideas. This cannot happen when you stay overly focused on a problem," explains Kaufman.[23]

Walking, in particular, appears to boost creativity. In a study appropriately titled *Give Your Ideas Some Legs*,[24] researchers found that, both during the walks and right afterward, people scored higher on several different creativity tests.

Kaufman clarifies that we should not stop focusing on the problem we are working or the solution we are seeking altogether; rather he encourages us to make room for unfocused and idle time *between periods of focused attention*. After all, insight does favor the prepared mind. Kaufman explains that, traditionally, creativity researchers believed there are three stages to creative problem solving:

- mastery, where you learn information and fine-tune your skills;
- inspiration, where you switch to a mindless task or enjoy some idle time;
- refinement, where you refocus on the original problem and re-engage in linear thinking to fine-tune your solution.

For example, when I was putting together this chapter, mastery helped me dive into the science of creativity, speaking to experts in the field and interviewing highly creative individuals. Inspiration came on hikes I took. During those times, the logic, flow, and sequencing of the chapter would effortlessly emerge. Refinement involved carefully editing the chapter to be as clear as possible for the reader.

Management experts Kimberly Elsbach and Andrew Hargadon[25] from the University of California, Davis suggest that—for maximum creativity—you should organize your workday schedule so that it alternates highly focused and demanding tasks with more mindless ones. Give yourself and those around you more room to breathe and a more diverse workload that alternates low-focus tasks (plugging in numbers, formatting a presentation, cleaning up your desk) with high-focus tasks (writing an article, preparing a PowerPoint presentation, leading a meeting).

Wharton professor Adam Grant warns us not to confuse tasks that are less intellectually demanding with tasks that are "leisurely."[26] For example, while we may think checking Facebook and reading a magazine are activities that rest our brains and allow us to enter an "idle state," they actually require a great deal of concentration. "What you want is partially focused attention," Grant explains. "For example, for a white-collar worker, if you can fill at least part of your day with data entry into a spreadsheet or that kind of task, it gets you into a rhythm and routine where you are only partly focused—making it more likely that you will think more clearly and innovatively later."[27]

Doing something boring to think more creatively sounds counterintuitive—but it works. When the mind is partially engaged, its resources are not overly taxed. It is free enough to forge unexpected, intriguing connections and to allow original ideas to bubble up to the surface.

Diversifying by Broadening Your Horizons

Diversification can also mean slightly broadening experiential and intellectual horizons. According to Kaufman, anything that violates expectations of how the world works can boost creativity. For example, a semester spent studying abroad boosts students' creativity. Why? New experiences that disrupt our usual way of life and show us a different perspective make us more mentally flexible or creative.

Myron Scholes—whose story opened this chapter—is an ardent believer in diversification.[28] Though he is an economist by training, Scholes doesn't spend day and night on math problems and market analysis. By reading widely outside of his academic field, he is able to apply principles from other disciplines, such as psychology, philosophy, and history, to his innovative analyses of human behavior. Scholes's secret is that he does not overconcentrate on a problem or limit himself to the study of one academic area, but instead spends time learning about other fields and engaging in activities that have nothing to do with his profession.

"You can't spread yourself too thin, but it is essential to diversify your interests. Of course, if you diversify completely, you get nothing.

But if you overconcentrate, you have no degrees of freedom," Scholes explains. "You need some concentration and some diversification."

Scholes's ideas that we need concentration and diversification might explain the fascinating dynamics behind Innocentive, a crowdsourcing platform. Innocentive crowdsources genius solutions to complex problems submitted by research and development companies—from creating car accessories to enhance the driving experience (a challenge submitted by Ford) to techniques for creating "earth independence," whereby humans are able to survive in space for longer periods (a challenge submitted by NASA). Anyone can submit a solution. Each challenge has a price tag attached. The winner can receive financial compensation in the range of $10,000 to $1 million.

A research study out of Harvard headed by Karim Lakhani[29] established that there was a higher probability of someone solving a problem submitted to Innocentive if that person was *not* an expert in that particular field, but was in a field that was marginally or not at all related. "The further the problem was from the solver's expertise," Lakhani shared with the *New York Times,* "the more likely they were to solve it."[30] In their paper, Lakhani and his team cite the example of a protein crystallography expert who was able to solve a toxicology problem that toxicologists could not figure out. Why? Because the methods she used—which were foreign to the toxicologists—were suited to cracking the problem. In fact, there was a 10 percent increased likelihood that someone would solve a challenge if his or her expertise was completely outside the challenge's field.

MAKE TIME FOR STILLNESS AND SILENCE

Given how busy modern life is, we can think of stillness and silence as another "diversifying" experience. Rather than being in motion and rushing from one place to the next, we are still. Rather than doing something, we do nothing. Rather than focusing on things, we completely unplug. Meditation is an obvious example of cultivating still-ness or silence.

Pico Iyer,[31] bestselling novelist and journalist for the *New York Times* and *Time* magazine whose TED talk has received over 2 million views, believes he is more creative when he has made time for stillness and introspection in his life—and that it's only when he is still that he can really be moved. He has even written a book on the subject entitled *The Art of Stillness.*

"The depth of my writing is in direct proportion to the depth of my silence," Iyer told me. "When I write fast information-filled pieces, readers respond in a fast information-filled way: they enjoy the ride and promptly forget everything. When I write in a 'quiet way' that is more still and contemplative, readers become more still and contem-plative themselves and the words and sentences have space to reso-nate." To consciously make room for stillness in his life and work, Iyer has gone 80 times over the past 24 years on retreat to a Benedictine hermitage. "I'm not specifically religious," he says. "I don't practice any formal religious meditation—stillness, silence, and space are what we need."

Research on silence provides insight into what makes silence so powerful and how it helps Iyer access his innate creativity. In 2006, Luciano Bernardi[32] was studying the impact of music on physiology. To his surprise, he found that not only did the music affect par-ticipants' physiology (slower music reduced heart rate, blood pressure, and breathing), but so did the moments of silence—which he had only included as a comparison measure.

In fact, Bernardi found that periods of silence inserted between tracks of music were much more relaxing than the soundtracks de-signed to induce relaxation or periods of silence administered without music in between. Physiologically, taking a "silence break" had the most profound relaxing and calming effect. Other studies have found that silence—despite being void of content—can help develop new brain cells.[33]

It may come as a surprise that silence, like activity, helps our brains develop, yet Iyer has found that removing himself from the bustle of society is key to thinking outside the box (and recalling what he cares for). The various demands placed on us, which rob us of the idle time we need to be creative—expectations that we will be available 24/7 and interruptions made possible by the various technologies we use every day—aren't going to go away. For Iyer, the solution lies not in changing those demands (which most of us can't anyway) but in altering our relationship to them—which is fundamentally an internal process.

"We can choose to step out of the permanent Times Square that is buzzing in our heads. Most people are noticing that they are drowning in it. And they are trying to find a way back to stillness: through hikes, sailing, meditation, Internet Sabbath," Iyer explains.

He believes his best work comes when he can hear something deeper than the clatter of the world. "When you stand about two inches away from the great canvas that is our world and our lives—just as when you stand too close to a painting—you can't catch the larger patterns in it, the meaning," Iyer explains. "When I go to my monastery in Big Sur, I spend a lot of time doing nothing, taking walks, lying on my bed—and I'm confident that it's only in that space that I will come up with something fresh and more interesting than my everyday ideas."

Stillness also allows him to step out of clock time into a more spacious sense of hours, which is of huge importance to his work as a writer. "As soon as I am in stillness, I can hear my deepest voice, everything that becomes inaudible when I am in constant motion."

But writers like Iyer are not the only ones who benefit from stillness to access their innate creativity. You wouldn't necessarily expect a skilled scientist, economist, and mathematician to derive creativity from a place of stillness. But Scholes does so through daily breathing exercises and meditation, as well as walks in nature and golf. He attributes much of his creative success to creating stillness around the problems he is dealing with, which allows new perspectives to emerge effortlessly. "It allows your mind to gather additional data and to challenge your own methodology," Scholes explains. "It gives you the ability to see other perspectives, let ideas percolate, challenge your views, gather additional data. You understand how unconnected things fit together."

To come up with new ways of thinking about things or doing things, we need to let ideas percolate, as Scholes describes. Taking quiet time that is undisturbed by other stimulation, information, or distraction is a way to optimally facilitate this creative process.

Silence can, of course, be uncomfortable. When your mind wanders, thoughts and feelings can emerge that are not necessarily pleasant. Being alone or being *un*busy or quiet can open the door to troublesome thoughts or even anxiety. You might even feel "stuck" on them, since the brain tends to focus on negative things. Yet if you sit through them, or walk through them (if your silent practice is a hike or a walk), you will see that they eventually pass, leaving room for free-flowing thoughts and daydreams. Just like any exercise, idle time will be more natural and enjoyable the more you engage in it.

INVITE FUN (AND HAPPINESS) BACK INTO YOUR LIFE

One of Scholes's and Iyer's most charming qualities is the lightness of their personalities. Each has a quick smile and an easy sense of humor. There is a childlike (though not childish) quality and playfulness about their curiosity and enthusiasm. This comes as no surprise. Another way to access our innate creativity is by having fun.

Filling idle time with fun and games is a natural part of children's lives. However, though engaging in playful activities for the sake of having fun exists in the animal kingdom (to which anyone with a pet can attest), it is completely neglected in human adulthood. We are the only adult mammals who do not make time for play, outside of highly structured settings like a Sunday neighborhood soccer game or playtime with a child.

Submerged in the responsibilities of life, the seriousness of world affairs, and an ever-growing to-do list, we often forget to play, feel we don't have time for it, or somehow believe it is no longer appropriate.

At Stanford, I helped found the first psychology of happiness course and led a session on the science of play. I decided to illustrate the effects of play on our emotions by introducing a grade-school game. We stood in a circle and whoever was "it" would stand in the middle. Participants would wink at each other in order to signal to each other to switch places in the circle. The person who was "it" would try to take their spot while they dashed to switch places. Although they stared at each other a little awkwardly at first, the college students soon jumped into the game with enthusiasm and laughter.

When I asked for feedback at the end of the game, students mentioned "feeling happy," "forgetting worries," and "being completely in the moment." One student, giddy with joy from the game, said, "I thought we weren't supposed to play anymore." She was seventeen.

At Stanford, many students have academic goals that make them feel like a hamster on a wheel—always on the go and hustling for success. As a consequence, playful activities fall by the wayside. As adults, we cast these kinds of activities aside as a childish and frivolous waste of time. However, they have tremendous potential to boost our creativity and our ability to think inventively, not to mention our well-being! After all, the root of the word *recreation* is *re-create*, "to refresh oneself by some amusement."[34]

Albert Einstein famously said, "To stimulate creativity, one must develop the childlike inclination for play." Although we adults may have lost the skill of playing with the innocence of a child, we can easily regain it. In one study,[35] undergraduate participants were divided into two groups before doing a creativity task. In one group, they were told to imagine that school was canceled and to write down a list of things they would do with their free day. In the other group, participants were given the same instruction but were asked to imagine that they were seven years old. The latter group came up with far more creative examples. This study shows us that our creative potential is not as buried as we think it is. It can be accessed easily just by using our, well, imagination.

Creative companies in a wide range of industries from technology to clothing understand the importance of play for employees' creativity. Google offices worldwide are built to foster playful creativity. In the Zurich office, for example, instead of walking places, you can take a fireman's pole or a slide to get from floor to floor. Facebook offers DJ mixing facilities alongside pool tables, as well as gaming opportunities. Alternative clothing company Comvert in Milan, Italy, converted an old theater into office space and turned the former audience seating area into a skateboard rink for employees.[36]

Play has a positive impact on creativity because—in addition to helping us both mind-wander and diversify—it stimulates positive emotion, which research shows leads to greater insight and better problem solving. Barbara Fredrickson of the University of North Carolina, Chapel Hill, found[37] that positive emotions increase our cognitive resources by expanding our visual attention. When we feel good, we gain the ability to pay attention to a wider range of experiences. We see the big picture rather than getting bogged down in the details. In other words, if you feel stuck in a rut or you can't think yourself out of a problem or don't see a way out of a situation, play may be a way of getting "unstuck" and coming up with innovative ideas.

Lolly Daskal[38] is a coach who consults with Fortune 500 companies. On one occasion, she was hired for a strategy session—to help a global leadership team figure out the mission, vision, and values for their company. Daskal made arrangements to get them out of their confined offices and held the strategy session in a beautiful space where there were lots of windows and views of nature. The idea was to stimulate their creative imagination. But despite the new location, the discussion was difficult, noncreative, and extremely linear. The team felt stuck. Daskal observed them talking in circles without coming up with a solution. That's when she decided to clear the air. She asked them all to stop working, stop thinking, and stop trying to come up with a solution.

She took them outside, where she had set up areas with different games to play. In one area she had dartboards, in another beanbags, and in yet another a whiffle ball and badminton rackets. She told the team to pick partners and to let go and have fun. They all welcomed the distraction, and before long they were all enjoying themselves. You could hear the lightness in their interactions and the joy of being free from the seriousness of that day.

After an hour or so, Daskal called them all back into the room, and they returned with high energy. Not only were they more relaxed, but they were ready to get back to work. This time, when Daskal asked, "What is this company all about?" answers kept coming and everyone was excited and eager to participate. The problem was resolved quickly and easily. By letting them enjoy themselves and having fun through play, Daskal helped them come up with the solution.

Just as joy and fun can make you more creative, creativity in turn enhances your well-being. The more creative you become, the more joy you invite into your life. Nikola Tesla wrote, "I do not think there is any thrill that can go through the human heart like that felt by the inventor as he sees some creation of the brain unfolding to success. . . . Such emotions make a man forget food, sleep, friends, love, everything." By naturally tapping into your inner creativity, you reconnect with the joy you had as a child playing. You engage in a positive feedback loop that continues to replenish you with joy and creativity. It makes for an adult life rich with delight and inventiveness.

This is where the research points: happiness is the secret to breakthrough creativity. Make sure to have idle time—but enjoy it. Treat it as time off, time for yourself, time to relax and have fun. Resist the urge for instant gratification. After all, expecting brilliance to emerge from an unstructured activity turns that activity into a purposeful one. Your mind returns to a state of focus and anxious expectation. For example, don't return from walking your dog thinking, "Gosh, I didn't have any creative insights about how to improve my presentation on this walk, and I missed the opportunity to call my bank to dispute that charge." You may find that creative insights arise on some occasions, and not on others. Either way, this period of integration and relaxation will benefit you more profoundly than you know.

MAKE TIME FOR IDLENESS

Although you may not think you have time for idleness or unstructured time, we all do. It doesn't always involve changing your schedule either. Sometimes it just means altering how you do things. Here are some examples of how you can diversify your activities, make time for stillness and silence, and engage in playful activities.

DIVERSIFY YOUR ACTIVITIES

- As Adam Grant[39] points out, we choose to pack any moment of unfocused nonworking time with some kind of focused consumption. On a break at work, you may check Google News, read up on the latest celebrity gossip, check your social media accounts, read your favorite blogs, or send some text messages. Instead, choose an activity that is less focused, like stretching, listening to music, taking a quick walk, or cleaning your desk.

- At work, organize your tasks so as to alternate activities that demand lots of concentration (for instance, writing up a proposal) with tasks that are less intellectually demanding (such as entering data). No matter what your profession, you will be able to identify the tasks that you find more or less challenging.

- If your work is mostly intellectual, you might learn some pragmatic skills to get out of your head: learn to change your car's oil, to cook Thai cuisine, to play an instrument, or to give a massage. If your job is more hands on or people oriented, diversification may mean studying a new language, learning chess, or reading poetry.

- Try expanding your areas of interest. Do you mostly read books or blogs about your field? If so, try switching to a whole different genre of reading materials: funny books, classics, or general-interest magazines. Watch TV shows or documentaries that have nothing to do with your primary field of work. If you enjoy social activities, join Meetup groups focused on activities you have never tried before, such as AcroYoga or cycling. Are you often sedentary, staying mostly in your office and car? Choose to exercise outside rather than spending time in an indoor gym—swim, go for hikes, ski.

MAKE TIME FOR SILENCE

- Sometimes we need a structured environment to unplug. Try attending a retreat; there are many meditation, wellness, yoga, and hiking retreats available. Start slowly if you are new to retreats. Try a day-long or weekend-long workshop.

- If retreats or meditation are not your thing, you can find silence in your own way. One opportunity for stillness that we have all around us is nature. Whether you're in a city or suburb, you can take a break from work and take a short stroll. Even in the thick of Manhattan, trees and plants are growing and birds and insects fly around. Nature is all around us, yet we often forget to notice. When you're out for a stroll, look up at the trees and the sky instead of checking your text messages. In fact, leave your phone behind.

- Meditation is a silent activity. There are many forms of meditation, some of which involve a lot of focus and concentration. If your life and profession already involves intense focus, you may wish to opt for a nonfocused meditation. Open awareness meditation and *suhuj samadhi* are examples of meditation that does not involve intense focus. Choose the type that feels right to you. Many workplaces now understand the benefits of this kind of activity and offer meditation or yoga classes that you can easily attend.

- You can introduce quiet time during mundane activities. Choose silence instead of listening to the radio while driving to work, eat your meals without having your computer open in front of you, fold your laundry without watching TV or making a phone call at the same time.

ENGAGE IN PLAY

- Remember what makes you laugh, whether it's attending a comedy show, watching slapstick films, or learning jokes. You could even join a laughter yoga group—workshops dedicated to laughing.

- Join a sports team (a structured activity, yes, but better than nothing!), or take a fun exercise class like pole dancing, trampoline, or trapeze.

- Engage in games that are fun for you. It could be board or card games, crosswords, or darts. Perhaps you love putting together model airplanes or building with Legos. Consider buying a Ping-Pong or pool table . . . and be careful not to turn that table into another place for competition and über-focus.

- Find a play partner. Animals and children are always ready to play and laugh. Find opportunities to play with your own children or pets or those of friends and family.

Finding time to engage in these activities may seem impossible, given how busy we are. Realize that doing so may require compromise on your part. Perhaps you won't stay on top of everything on your to-do list; perhaps you'll have to say no to those who demand access to you 24/7. But the payoff for your professional and personal success is huge and well worth it.

Creativity and the success it produces do not emerge out of single-minded focus on "purposeful" activities. They come from idleness, fun, stillness, calm, and relaxation. It may seem counterintuitive that taking a walk, relaxing on your porch, reading a novel rather than an article related to your field, or doing something fun like playing a round of golf can help you develop better ideas and come up with creative solutions to problems. Yet it is through these acts of self-care and enjoyment that your greatest insights are likely to occur. The heightened levels of psychological well-being you will derive from being idle, diversifying your activities, and finding time for silence and play can greatly contribute to your success.

FIVE

ENJOY A SUCCESSFUL RELATIONSHIP . . . WITH YOURSELF

HOW YOU RELATE TO YOURSELF AFFECTS YOUR POTENTIAL

When I let go of what I am, I become what I might be.

—*Lao Tzu*

My friend Laura seemed to have it all: she was blonde, beautiful, athletic, radiant, and brilliant; she was one of those rare students who made all As and A+s at Yale. She appeared to be the epitome of success. In an academically gifted student body, she stood a head above everyone else.

Two years into her college experience, despite all her accomplishments, Laura dropped out.

Laura had the skills and motivation to do well at Yale, but how she perceived herself was standing in the way of success. Laura had always been an A student—that's who she was for as long as she could remember. She felt she had to achieve perfection and had an immense fear of failure, so she took only classes she knew would result in good grades. When she didn't do well or struggled to get top marks in all her classes—as was bound to eventually happen in college—she was tough on herself in an effort to motivate herself to try harder and stay focused. Fueled by these beliefs, Laura achieved perfect grades—and perfect misery. "I remember feeling gnarled and self-critical all of the time," Laura told me. She ended up suffering from levels of depression and anxiety so high that she could no longer sustain a college career.

What distinguishes those who thrive in the face of life's difficulties and professional challenges from those who become demoralized? Their relationship with themselves. In particular their beliefs about themselves and the way they treat themselves.

The truth is that most of us are not kind to ourselves in our quest for success. We've been taught that to be successful, *we need to play to our strengths,* so we had better find out the things that we are innately good at and stick to them—because we are unlikely to overcome our weaknesses. If I am bad at math, I probably shouldn't go into accounting or engineering. If I'm not a people person, I had better stay out of sales. And when we do run up against our weaknesses, we feel that *we have to be self-critical.* Self-criticism will keep us honest about our shortcomings and ensure we stay motivated and on our toes. By always demanding better of ourselves, we'll do our best.

Recent scientific research suggests that these ideas are myths. There is no doubt that knowing your strengths and weaknesses *is* a good idea. However, the way you approach them can set you up either for success or for failure. The way you view yourself (do you believe your strengths are limited?) and the way you respond to failures (are you your worst critic, or can you treat yourself as you would a friend?) have a tremendous impact on your personal and professional lives.

Understanding that you can build new strengths rather than limiting yourself to the ones you perceive that you have and being self-compassionate rather than self-critical will help you to be resilient in the face of failure, to learn and grow from your mistakes, and to discover opportunities you otherwise would never have found. As a consequence, you will feel grateful, be far happier, and your chances for success will increase manifold.

THE PERILS OF PLAYING TO YOUR STRENGTHS

We generally assume that what distinguishes extraordinary people, such as star singers, bestselling authors, famous movie actors, or self-made billionaires from the rest of us is their particular *strengths*. We think these people have a special gift. They may have a knack for business or an artistic bent or some other "it factor." We believe their inherent strengths set them apart and therefore make them successful. Conversely, if the rest of us don't reach their heights, it is because we lack such gifts. You've either got "it"—whatever "it" may be—or you don't, and there's not much that you can do about it.

We think about our own strengths in similar ways. For example, you might think of yourself as a math person or not, a people person or not, a creative person or not. Ultimately, you believe, your success is predestined by the natural abilities and gifts you are fortunate to have. You simply play the hand you're dealt.

This belief that we are born with certain innate strengths that determine what we can and cannot achieve, however, severely backfires on us—especially in times of failure or challenge. Carol Dweck, Stanford University developmental psychologist, has been conducting research for decades on the self-beliefs of children and adults. Early in her career, Dweck noticed that schoolchildren faced with failure to solve a difficult math problem could have two completely different reactions: Either they lose motivation and give up—and therefore don't learn anything new. Or they keep going with increased enthusiasm—and thereby gain new skills. What determines their reaction? If they believe in natural strengths—that is, if they subscribe to the false theory of success I described earlier—and they aren't able to solve the problem, they figure that they just don't have the skills for it and give up. Not only do they not learn whatever lesson the math problem was supposed to impart—but they also feel worse about their math abilities and themselves.

Over decades of research across a wide array of failure scenarios, Dweck showed that the psychological phenomenon she had observed in children is pervasive and equally debilitating no matter what your age. When faced with a challenge or failure—a new skill set, a relationship, a job—you may simply assume that you don't have the talent for it. In the face of failure, you give up and your emotional well-being takes a hit. Why is that?

Believing in *strengths* leads to the following kind of logic: "If I fail to successfully put together a financial model, it reveals that finance is not a strength of mine. I should probably not work in finance." Having pigeonholed yourself as "not good" at the particular task you failed at, you feel hopeless about your abilities in that area, preventing you from learning from your mistake and developing new skills. If you stop persevering in anything outside the areas you are good at, you simply cannot expand your sphere of knowledge or competence.

This belief system can be particularly damaging professionally if, for example, you work in a field that is always changing and evolving—which many of us are doing. For example, if your industry is expanding to China or Japan, you may want to learn these languages. However, if you believe that languages are not one of your strengths, you won't even try. Your belief, of course, becomes a self-fulfilling prophecy. Chances are that your knowledge and skill set will forever remain limited to the areas of your life that you see as strengths.

Of course, this is not to say you should *not* engage in work that comes easily to you or suits your natural inclinations. But research has persuasively shown that you shouldn't let yourself believe that you are *limited* to being good at the activities that come easily for you. You may have enormous potential waiting to be uncovered.

Had R. H. Macy assumed he was not made for business after the first five stores he created failed, he would never have founded the wildly successful Macy's stores. Had Bill Gates assumed that computer start-ups were not for him after his first company, Traf-O-Data, went under, he would never have founded Microsoft. Had Theodor Seuss Geisel, otherwise known as the celebrated children's writer Dr. Seuss, concluded that he was not a good author after his first manuscript was rejected over twenty times, he would never have revolutionized children's literature.

Perhaps more importantly, when you believe in *strengths* alone and you aren't successful—not getting into your first choice university, not getting that job you wanted, not getting the promotion you thought you deserved, not being in a good relationship—you are devastated. You become hopeless because you assume you can't progress in those areas. Unsurprisingly, research shows that subscribing to the idea of *strengths* is linked to higher levels of depression,[1] probably in part because it leads to excessive self-criticism.

THE DANGERS OF HARSH SELF-CRITICISM

While it may seem obvious that harsh self-criticism can be destructive, we tend to engage in it quite frequently in the belief that it will do us good. "I'm lazy," "I give up too easily," "I'm not smart enough." We're often our own worst critics. We also believe that self-criticism pushes us to perform better and to live up to higher standards. After all, if we don't keep ourselves in check, who will? Some people even pride themselves on how "hard-core" and "persistent" they are. They wear the fact that they don't cut themselves any slack like a badge of honor. Like Laura, most of us don't stop to question our self-critical habit. We may not even notice it. And if we do, we likely don't bother to question its effect on us.

Research shows, however, that when you are excessively self-critical, you damage both your psychological well-being and your chances at success. Kristin Neff, associate professor of human development at the University of Texas, points out that self-criticism is an important predictor of anxiety and depression[2] and, rather than being a motivator, it can actually prevent you from trying again after failure for fear of failing once more.

Our brains have competing systems: one that seeks rewards and another that fears failure.[3] Fear of failure, when excessive, stands directly in the way of success:

- **It hurts your performance.** Research on athletes shows that, like a self-fulfilling prophecy, fear of failure leads them to "choke"—to fail at the critical point, such as a runner who trips during the race for which he has been preparing for months.[4]

- **It makes you give up.** Fear of mistakes and failure can make us so insecure and anxious that we give up early when faced with challenges. After all, if we fail, we will be faced with a barrage of harsh self-criticism.[5]

- **It leads to poor decision making.** Studies show that fear of failure can make you so anxious that you become less interested in learning and more willing to take shortcuts like cheating.[6] A study with entrepreneurs shows that those with a strong fear of failure are more likely to overlook potential investors' unethical behavior and to enter a dubious partnership with them regardless.[7]

- **It makes you lose touch with what you really want.** Your fear of failing can even lead you to lose touch with the kind of career path you wish to pursue. My friend Laura told me that, by focusing more on performance and less on her personal interests, choosing classes where she could get good grades over topics she enjoyed, she disconnected from herself and lost touch with her real preferences. "This made transitioning to the workplace hard for me because I didn't know what I was interested in," Laura explains. "I also found that at work I didn't receive a regular report card with grades. It took me about five-plus years to reach any kind of professional satisfaction, and that was only after a series of false starts."

Not only can self-criticism increase fear of failure, but being our own worst critics also makes us focus on what's *wrong* with us—which takes a psychological toll. As described in an earlier chapter it is far easier to focus on the negative: research shows that the brain has a *negativity bias.* Our perspective is biased toward the negative; as far as our minds are concerned, bad is stronger than good. Research by Roy Baumeister[8] and others suggests that this tendency to give more weight to the negative may have helped our species survive by highlighting potential dangers. However, in this day and age, our negativity bias, both as it relates to the environment and to our self-judgments, is harmful.

We have such a strong propensity to favor *negativity* that we have a skewed vision of reality. An analysis[9] by Shelley Gable and Jonathan Haidt suggests that while we have three times more positive experiences than negative, we tend to focus on the negative ones. This research suggests that, if we were able to see things as they really are, we would actually have a *positivity bias,* because 75 percent of our lives is going relatively well. However, we live our lives so focused on the negative that we often fail to notice, let alone enjoy, what we do have.

People have a similar tendency when it comes to themselves. Your relationship with yourself is self-critical because you focus on your faults and weaknesses. If you are facing an end-of-year performance evaluation, you may notice that during your self-evaluation you remember the project you botched, reports that didn't go well, or that time you had an unfortunate interaction with your boss. If, to your surprise, your manager praises you for a long list of things you did well this year but mentions one or two that he wished you had done differently, you are still probably going to focus on the negative feedback.

Another tendency that reinforces our negativity bias is taking our achievements for granted. If your goal has been to become a great researcher or writer or chef, you may have worked for years to get there. However, when you reach your goal, you'll find that you're still not satisfied. Why? Because in addition to focusing on the negative, we also get used to the good things in our lives and start to take them for granted—a phenomenon called habituation. While you may receive a boost of happiness from, say, a meritorious promotion or public recognition like an award in your field, over time these events lose their ability to bring you renewed joy because you become accustomed to them.

Given our propensity toward negativity, a self-critical habit only further reinforces this negativity, skewing our image of ourselves and further endangering success and happiness. Now, I'm not saying that you should ignore your shortcomings to avoid self-criticism. If you have a tendency to procrastinate that leads you to miss important deadlines, damages the quality of your work, or increases your stress, for example, you may want to reflect on how you can address this habit. There is a difference between self-awareness—understanding your weaknesses— and harsh self-criticism, which only adds pressure to an already stressful situation and in fact prevents you from achieving your best.

If believing that success depends on your strengths on the one hand, and your tendency to self-criticize on the other ends up sabotaging your chances of success, then how can you change your self-beliefs to make them more productive? Research suggests you should replace your belief in strengths with effort, and self-criticism with self-compassion.

BELIEVE IN EFFORT, NOT STRENGTHS

Albert Einstein, despite being called a genius, simply did not buy into the *strengths* idea: "Failure is success in progress," he is quoted as saying. Einstein rightly understood that strengths do not just happen, they need to be *developed*.

It was a good thing that Einstein subscribed to those beliefs. As a child, he was so slow in learning to speak and write that his family thought he might be mentally handicapped. Later, he was expelled from school and failed to gain admittance to Zurich Polytechnic School. When he finally did finish university, he was the only one in his class who did not land a teaching position. Had Einstein believed in the *strengths* theory, he would have assumed that he did not have what it took to be a scientist. However, because he believed that his skills could *develop,* he did not let the failures stop him but went on to revolutionize physics, eventually winning a Nobel Prize.[10]

Neuroscientific data clearly demonstrates that our brains continue to grow new neuronal pathways throughout life. The brain is designed for development and to learn new things. While particular skills may come more easily, we are wired to engage, thrive, and grow in any number of areas, from playing the violin to learning to drive a stick shift, from mastering Chinese calligraphy to excelling on the Certified Public Accountant exam.

So what determines whether we learn new skills? In large part, our beliefs. Dweck's research shows that the big difference between those who persist in the face of failure and those who don't is whether they *be-*

lieve they can *develop* strengths (rather than being born with them). They understand that, with persistence, they can improve at anything. As a consequence, they learn from their mistakes, are more emotionally resilient in the face of failure, and ultimately achieve more and with greater self-confidence.[11] A challenge, a problem, or a mistake they face does not define them but rather is an adventure to get excited about, a wonderful opportunity for learning and growth. When I was a graduate student at Stanford, Dweck shared with us the words of a boy who, when he failed the difficult math problem in Dweck's study, enthusiastically went back to working on the problem, saying, "I *love* a challenge!"

Jack Ma was born to a poor family in Hangzhou, in China's Zhejiang Province. He failed his university entrance exams not once but twice before being admitted to Hangzhou Teachers' Institute. After completing his studies, he applied for dozens of jobs, for which he was categorically rejected. He finally became an English teacher making a humble salary of $12 a month. As part of a translation job, he traveled to the United States and discovered the Internet. Inspired, he founded two Internet start-ups that failed. He persisted and founded Alibaba Shareholdings. Today he is the richest man in China,[12] with an estimated worth of $25 billion.[13] He is executive chairman of Alibaba and was recently nominated by *Time* as one of the "most influential people of 2009."[14]

Had Ma held a *strengths* perspective, he would have stuck to what he knew best: teaching English. After all, Ma had never written a line of code or made even a single sale to a customer before deciding to launch a commercial Internet venture. But Ma derived his enthusiasm from the belief that if he failed, he would have learned from the experience. "No matter what one does, regardless of failure or success, the experience is a form of success in itself. You have got to keep trying, and if it doesn't work, you always can revert back to what you were doing before," Ma said.[15]

As Ma's story shows, your self-perspective has the power to determine your overall well-being, confidence, and success. It foretells whether you will bounce back and thrive in the face of inevitable failure. It also predicts whether you will take a challenge and embark on new opportunities, developing new skills along the way.

In these new ventures, we will inevitably encounter new setbacks. When these start showing up, withholding self-criticism and engaging in a more positive relationship with ourselves further strengthens our chances at success.

THE POWER OF SELF-COMPASSION

Laura realized that she needed to change her attitude about herself and confront her overtly self-critical behavior despite the social pressure to tough it out. At the time, she told me, "I have to leave so I can learn to loosen the reins on myself." Many of us don't ever reach the wise realization she did so young. Instead we aspire to have *tighter* reins and a stronger whip for ourselves, with the idea that we should expect more and more of ourselves.

After leading a self-destructive life, Laura put a stop to the excessively self-critical demands she had placed on herself. She developed a gentler approach that involved more friendliness to herself, greater leniency toward her own shortcomings, and a broader and more mindful perspective. In sum, she became what researchers call "self-compassionate."

Rather than being driven solely by external motivations, focusing her attention and energy outwards on academic or athletic goals alone, she developed awareness of her own needs and was kind to herself when she faced setbacks. Soon her radiant smile reappeared. She continued to excel, but no longer at the price of her own well-being.

Scientific evidence supports what Laura figured out intuitively: self-compassion is one of the most fundamental determinants of resilience and success. Where excessive self-criticism can leave us weak and distraught, self-compassion is at the heart of empowerment.

What exactly is self-compassion? Self-compassion involves treating yourself as you would treat a colleague or friend who has failed. Rather than berating and judging, thereby adding to your friend's despair, you listen with understanding. You encourage your friend to remember that mistakes are normal. Neff[16] pioneered research on self-compassion and has outlined its three components:

- **Being kind to yourself.** Self-compassion involves treating oneself with understanding and patience rather than using shaming, criticism, or harsh reprimands. It involves engaging in a positive and encouraging internal dialogue with yourself. Neff suggested the following kinds of phrases: "It's okay that you failed; it doesn't mean you're a bad person or bad at what you do," "I believe in you and support you, and I know you can do it," "I'd like you to try to make a change so you can be happier."

- **Understanding that you are part of humanity, that everyone makes mistakes.** "To err is human," wrote Alexander Pope. Knowing that everyone confronts failure sooner or later helps you be less critical and upset when it's your turn. You reframe failure as a normal occurrence and therefore are less shaken by it. You remind yourself that "this can happen to anyone" and that "everyone fails sometimes" and that "failure is the best learning experience." You come to realize that there are areas of your professional or personal life in which you still need to grow or develop greater skills, and you set about your day with renewed resolve to address those weaknesses.

- **Mindfulness.** Mindfulness is being aware of and validating your thoughts and feelings, yet observing them with perspective and distance and without overidentifying with them. Instead of succumbing to a torrent of emotion, including anger at yourself, just observe the thoughts and feelings that come up as you would observe a storm from your window. Mindfulness does not mean suppressing or denying these feelings, but rather being present with them as they are. Neff suggested the following examples of a mindful approach to thoughts and feelings: "This is really hard right now," "I'm sorry you are struggling," and "this moment will pass."

As the science director of Stanford's Center for Compassion and Altruism Research and Education, I know all too well that a word which includes *compassion* can, at first impression, sound "soft" or idealistic. But self-compassion is anything but soft—it's smart. It allows you to be successful without sabotaging yourself.

Self-compassion does not mean, for example, letting yourself off the hook when you fail or make mistakes. It simply means that you approach these setbacks in a more constructive way, learning from them instead of beating yourself up because of them. Self-compassion also does not mean that you don't recognize your weaknesses. In one study, Neff found that when faced with a threatening situation—a job interview in which they were asked to describe their "biggest weakness"—people with higher self-compassion used as many negative descriptions of themselves as did people with low self-compassion. However, self compassionate people experienced far less anxiety as a result of the task.[17] Neff showed in other studies that self-compassion makes you resilient regardless of the praise or criticism you receive.[18] In other words, because you feel fine about both your positive and negative attributes, you aren't as influenced and vulnerable to other people's opinions.

Neff's research demonstrates that by engaging in self-compassion, we bring out the best in ourselves. Self-compassion—as opposed to self-criticism—helps people thrive[19] and is associated with a host of benefits:

- greater psychological well-being;
- less anxiety, depression, and stress;[20]
- more happiness, optimism, curiosity, creativity, and positive emotions;[21]
- better health;
- lower cellular inflammation in response to stress;[22]
- reduced cortisol[23] (a stress-related hormone);
- increased heart rate variability, a physiological marker associated with the ability to bounce back faster from stressful situations;[24]
- improved professional and personal skills;
- stronger motivation;[25]
- better relationships with other people;[26]
- reduced fear of failure and greater willingness to try again;[27]
- enhanced willpower;[28]
- greater perspective and reduced tendency to become overwhelmed during times of struggle.[29]

Though further research into the physiology of self-compassion versus excessive self-criticism is still pending, compassion researchers like Paul Gilbert have hypothesized a simple model. Harsh self-criticism activates the sympathetic (fight-or-flight) nervous system and elevates stress hormones like cortisol. When this sting has a hold on us, we cannot learn from or engage with the kernel of truth that may be there to serve us. Self-compassion, on the other hand, triggers the mammalian care-giving system and hormones of affiliation and love, such as oxytocin. Also known as the "cuddle hormone," oxytocin is released during hugging, sex, and in lactating mothers. It is associated with feelings of well-being.[30] We can engage with feedback we receive and learn from it without being destroyed by it.

The hardest part about self-compassion is to counter our tendency to focus on the negative. As a consequence of the negativity, bias, and habituation, it is much easier to be self-critical. There is one habit, however, that prevents us from succumbing to this tendency: gratitude. Gratitude balances our negativity bias by making us more aware of positive experiences in life and helping us focus on the positive aspects about ourselves. Gratitude helps us adopt a more balanced view that bolsters our happiness and success.

Congressman Tim Ryan of Ohio is the youngest congressman ever elected to Congress.[31] Voted into office in 2003 at age twenty-nine, he embodies the happiness track to success I describe in this book. He lives true to his values and passionately advocates for causes he believes in, even when they do not confer a political advantage. When you meet Congressman Ryan, you see a man who not only is successful, but also deeply fulfilled, contented, and joyful.

However, Congressman Ryan's daily dealings are not without their challenges. "The world can be—if you see it that way—a negative place. How do you stop yourself from getting overwhelmed when you're out in the world (whether in DC politics or office politics) and the knives are out and people are unkind and trying to hurt you?" As a congressman, whatever decisions Ryan makes in Congress inevitably bring upon him a slew of harsh criticism and attacks from his opponents.

"Given the negativity that comes at you—and sometimes it's really hard—you really have to stop and breathe. It's important to operate from a place of gratitude and thankfulness and appreciation for what you have." Rather than being defeated, self-critical, or angry when he is attacked, Congressman Ryan is able to turn the negativity that is directed his way into gratitude. Gratitude is the most self-compassionate act possible when faced with so much hostility. It provides him with the level-headedness and calm to keep going and to troubleshoot situations appropriately. Gratitude is a source of great strength.

Research supports the idea that gratitude has tremendous benefits; gratitude not only boosts your well-being but also significantly strengthens professional skills.

Greater psychological well-being and health:

- improved positive emotion[32]
- longer-lasting positive emotion[33]
- buffering against stress and negativity[34]
- decreased anxiety and depression[35]
- reduced materialism[36] (and materialism is linked to lower levels of well-being[37])
- improved sleep quality and duration, in part because you have more grateful thoughts before you go to sleep[38]

Improved professional skills:

- higher social intelligence[39]
- improved relationships[40]
- likeability (gratitude makes you a kinder, more altruistic, moral, and ethical person)[41]
- strengthened willpower[42]
- better long-term decision making[43]
- increased positive influence on others, who become more ethical and act with greater integrity[44] and greater kindness[45]

Despite the benefits of gratitude, a significant gratitude gap exists in America. Only 52 percent of women and 44 percent of men express gratitude to others on a regular basis.[46] Given this sad fact, how often are we actually grateful to *ourselves*? Every day, we have a choice about how we interpret our lives. We have the choice to either focus on what we want and don't yet have (say, better work habits), thereby feeling down. Or we can focus on what we do have (say, loyalty and integrity). Every one of us has at least one aspect of ourselves (and probably many more!) for which we can be grateful. When we take note of our positive qualities and are grateful for them, we become more self-compassionate—not to mention that we start to see ourselves in a much more realistic and positive light.

Some people have a difficult time feeling grateful because they are so worn down by the difficulties and challenges they face. An interesting study[47] showed that whether you derive happiness from everyday ordinary events or only from extraordinary events depends on your perception of the remaining time you have to live. The less time you perceive yourself as having, the more pleasure you derive from the simplest of things. Analogous research with the elderly and college students in their *last semester* (an end being in sight for both of these populations) found that they too are more likely to appreciate common experiences.

Most of us live as if we have an infinite number of tomorrows. Not until we get ill or someone close to us passes away do we awaken to the impermanence of life. Finiteness brings bittersweet poignancy to this moment because this moment will never come again. Although some find this idea depressing, in truth it is a call to action. We can choose to celebrate our lives and ourselves. No matter what challenges are thrown our way, it is up to us whether we will embrace the gifts that life brings to us and that we bring to it—or be blind to them. Our ability to be grateful for this moment will make us not only happier but more successful to boot.

"The happiest people don't have the best of everything, but they make the best of everything they have" goes the saying. When you notice harsh self-criticism and the negativity bias in your mind, closing your eyes and remembering the aspects of yourself for which you feel grateful will provide a reality check and prevent you from feeling down about yourself; it will help you see yourself as you really are. As for your weaknesses, addressing them from a place of self-compassion will help you thrive. Similarly, remembering to reflect on what is going well in your life helps you counter habituation so you keep celebrating all the ways you are fortunate. Sure, there will always be difficult situations and plenty to grouse about. However, you can either let these situations control your mind and take a real toll on your well-being and professional aspirations, or you can take charge. The situations may not change, but you can.

HOW TO BECOME MORE SELF-COMPASSIONATE

Self-compassion can seem challenging. Not only are we used to being self-critical, but we are brought up to avoid bragging. We are taught to be kind to others, but the idea of being kind to oneself can seem foreign or even new-agey. As we've discussed, however, there are solid scientific reasons why self-compassion is good for you and your career. Here are some tips for how to make self-compassion a habit.

Notice your self-talk. Neff suggests that in times of failure or challenge, noticing your self-talk can help you curb self-criticism and replace it with self-compassion. For example, instead of saying things like "How could I have done this? I'm such an idiot!" you might say, "I had a moment of absent-mindedness and that's okay. It could have happened to anyone; it's no big deal."

Write yourself a letter. When your emotions are overwhelming, Neff suggests writing a letter to yourself as if you were writing to a friend. Let's say you made a costly error and are feeling angry with yourself. It might feel stilted or strange at first, but write a letter as if you were writing it to someone dear to you who had committed the same error. Your words should comfort and not attack, normalizing the situation rather than blowing it out of proportion. A number of studies demonstrate that writing about your emotions can help regulate them.[48]

Develop a self-compassion phrase. Neff suggests developing a self-compassion mantra or phrase that you can turn to in challenging situations, so you can deal with them calmly and with grace. Her mantra is "This is a moment of suffering. Suffering is part of life. May I be kind to myself in this moment; may I give myself the compassion I need."

Make a daily gratitude list. Write down five things you feel grateful for every day. Again—this may sound overly simplistic. However, this extremely short exercise can produce powerful and long-lasting results.[49] To increase your self-compassion, at the end of each day, write down five things you are proud of having accomplished or five positive qualities you see in yourself.

After leaving Yale, my friend Laura took a year off to get in touch with herself, reflecting on what she truly wanted and learning to release the excessively tight leash she had on herself. She participated in a wilderness expedition program and worked at a bookstore that specialized in mystery novels—a genre she loved. After her year-long hiatus, she transferred to another Ivy League university in her hometown to live close to the nurturing environment of her family home. After graduation, two highly selective law schools offered her merit-based full scholarships. She currently works at a federal agency in Washington, DC, and is happily married. She is adamant about not passing on the false parameters of success that once devastated her life: "I don't want my daughters to feel the same suffocation that I felt, hyperventilating when any grade lower than an A was a possibility."

Could Laura have succeeded at Yale had she "toughed it out," continuing to be her own worst critic and relentlessly driving herself to excel? Perhaps. But at what cost? And how long would that success last before she inevitably burned out completely? By fundamentally changing her relationship with herself—both how she perceived her strengths and weaknesses and how she treated herself—Laura was able to find well-being *and* a sustainable path to success.

That's the power of self-compassion and of believing that talents and strengths can be developed. Not only do they build your inner strength by creating a strong and stable foundation at the level of your mind, but they ensure that you will continue to flourish over the long term.

SIX

UNDERSTAND THE KINDNESS EDGE

WHY COMPASSION SERVES YOU
BETTER THAN SELF-INTEREST

Goodness is the only investment that never fails.

—Henry David Thoreau[1]

When Drake[2] first joined the Wall Street investment bank Bear Stearns as a managing director, he was immediately taken aback by its self-interested culture. The investment banking industry is no doubt competitive and intense. But Drake, who had previously worked at an investment bank where collegiality and collaboration were highly valued, found Bear Stearns to be particularly harsh. "It was the worst culture I have ever experienced on Wall Street," he told me. Bear Stearns was "not able to compete on the hiring front against firms like Morgan Stanley and Goldman Sachs, who were more elite establishments," Drake explained, so its culture was "scrappy, independent, aggressive—it was the 'kids who came from the other side of the tracks' type of culture."

Drake explained that Bear Stearns liked to keep its operating costs low and pay higher bonuses to employees. As a managing director, if you generated business, you would get a significantly higher payout than at any other bank. As a consequence, Drake's fellow managing directors were so competitive that they often did not greet each other in the hallways or demonstrate any genuine interest in forging relationships. They were steadfastly looking out for themselves alone, were aggressively secretive about their clients, and were prone to take credit for their colleagues' deals.

Bear Sterns's culture may seem particularly cutthroat, but it represents an exaggerated version of a theory of success that is deeply embedded in our culture: to be successful, first and foremost you have to look out for yourself. We are taught that it's a dog-eat-dog, sink-or-swim, everyone-for-himself world, so you need to focus on number one so you are not outrun by the competition. In childhood, we are taught about the idea of survival of the fittest. And economists, who have long argued that our primary motivation is self-interest, have propagated the idea that we are all selfish creatures. Resources are limited, they tell us, so you have to fight off the competition and look out for your own interests.

Can you outperform your classmates to get into a better college? Once you start work, are you going to get promoted, or will your colleague get the position instead? In business, can you outdo the competition? It seems obvious that you've got to stay focused on "me, myself, and I." It's a zero-sum game; there's one winner and one loser, so you'd better win.

Scientific research, however, shows that being selfish and self-focused can actually prevent you from being as successful as you could be. Those who make compassion—not self-interest—a priority in their dealings with others are more likely to be happy and successful, as well as helping others succeed.

The notion of "survival of the fittest"—often misattributed to Charles Darwin—was in fact coined by a political theorist, Herbert Spencer, who wanted to justify social and economic hierarchies.[3]

Darwin, by contrast, argued that "communities, which included the greatest number of the most sympathetic members, would flourish best, and rear the greatest number of offspring."[4] Compassion and kindness are the actual cause of our survival over the centuries. We need to help others survive and thrive both in nature and in our lives.

WHY SELF-FOCUS BACKFIRES

In 2008, after the subprime mortgage market collapsed, Bear Stearns went down with it. Drake told me that while other factors played a role in Bear Stearns's demise, its greedy and self-interested reputation did not help. Bear Stearns's CEO at the time, James "Jimmy" Cayne—who personified a spirit of self-interest and aggression—was part of the problem.[5]

"Jimmy was arrogant and didn't have many friends on Wall Street," Drake explained. "When Long Term Capital Management LP, a hedge fund management firm, failed in 1998, Jimmy and Bear Stearns told the Federal Reserve and other heads of Wall Street that they were not going to participate in the bailout.[6] So guess what? When Bear needed a bailout, no one was willing to help. In fact, everyone sat there waiting to scoop up a highly profitable franchise as soon as the Federal Reserve rid it of the toxic subprime mortgage mess."

In March 2008, the Federal Reserve Bank ended up providing an emergency loan to prevent the collapse of the bank under the condition that it would sell to J. P. Morgan over the weekend. Bear Stearns's shares—once priced at $171.50[7]—were sold to J. P. Morgan Chase for $10 each.

As exemplified by the story of Bear Stearns, a self-interested approach may get results in the short term, but over the long term it ends up failing you. And in some extreme cases, it can cost you *everything*. Research suggests that self-focus harms you in four ways: it creates blind spots, ruins your relationships, makes you weak in the face of failure, and damages your health.

SELF-FOCUS CREATES BLIND SPOTS

Self-focus can lead to a type of hubris or, in psychological terms, narcissism. Narcissism, according to Jean Twenge, professor at San Diego State University and coauthor of *The Narcissism Epidemic,* is an inflated feeling of superiority and entitlement: "It's a multifaceted trait that brings together vanity, materialism, lack of empathy, relationship problems, egotism. It's a big, complex umbrella of traits, but at its core is that inflated sense of self." While many of us believe we are not narcissistic, an alarming survey by Twenge indicates that narcissism scores are on the rise. The narcissism scores of college students have climbed steeply since 1987, with 65 percent of modern-day students scoring higher in narcissism than previous generations.[8]

Twenge[9] told me in an interview that when her study first came out, many college newspapers wrote opinion pieces and articles about the findings. To her surprise, most of these articles did not disagree at all with the findings. However, they argued that they *have* to be narcissists to be successful in a competitive world. "The premise is that narcissism will help you succeed," explains Twenge. "But the problem with that premise is that it doesn't."

One reason narcissists end up failing is that they take too many risks, Twenge explains, because they don't have a clear view of their own abilities. As a consequence, narcissism leads to poorer performance over the long term. Particularly in the workplace, narcissism can result in incredible blind spots, leading you to see your leadership and professional skills in a far more positive light than your supervisor sees them. This kind of excessive positive regard can make you blind to your own weaknesses.[10]

In terms of leadership, Twenge explains that narcissists always want to be leaders, but that once in place, they are disliked by their teams and remain ineffective. We generally prefer leaders who are humble, agreeable, and compassionate, she points out. There is one exception to this rule, Twenge acknowledges. When it comes to public performances—occasions when other people are watching—narcissists tend to do well, but in most other arenas, from business to education, narcissists fare poorly.

SELF-FOCUS RUINS YOUR RELATIONSHIPS

Self-focus and narcissism can harm your relationships and drive people away, Twenge shared with me. We probably all know colleagues or managers who are overly enamored with themselves. It's either overt they boast about their accomplishments and seek the limelight—or more subtle, as they manipulate situations to get the credit for other people's work. This is an all-too-common scenario in academia, for example, where some scientists and professors routinely take the recognition for work that is actually conducted by graduate students and postdoctoral scientists.

Chances are we won't enjoy spending time with that person, nor—most important—do we trust them as colleagues or leaders. People who are looking out for themselves first may very well throw you under the bus if it serves their interests.

It's no surprise that excessive narcissism and self-centeredness can ruin relationships. Narcissists are prone to harsh behavior because when their self-esteem is threatened or they believe they are not given due respect, they tend to respond with anger and aggression.[11] A workplace study entitled "Narcissism and Counterproductive Work Behavior: Do Bigger Egos Mean Bigger Problems?" showed that people who rank high on the narcissism scale also rank high in anger and counterproductive work behavior. They were more likely to engage in unethical acts that harmed the organization, including interpersonal aggression, theft, sabotage, wasting time, spreading rumors, and slowing down work.[12] Narcissists can become biased against others and even engage in bullying behavior to feel good about themselves.[13] What's more, the social isolation that inevitably arises around them ends up exacerbating their antisocial behavior, leading to further isolation.[14]

This anger and bullying further damage their relationships. Research shows that anger and frustration erode the loyalty of colleagues and employees. Wharton professor Adam Grant[15] points out that if you are unkind to someone, they are likely to reciprocate; if you treat a colleague or employee with anger, their reaction may come back to haunt you. "Next time you need to rely on that employee, you may have lost some of the loyalty that was there before," says Grant.

Moreover, managers who express negative emotions like anger are seen as less effective.[16] Self-centered managers typically put undue pressure on their teams—which initiates a stress response that negatively affects employers and employees alike. In a study of employees from various organizations, health-care expenditures for those with high levels of stress were 46 percent greater than at similar organizations without high levels of stress.[17] Research also shows that workplace stress can lead to high turnover, as employees look for new jobs, decline promotions, or even quit.[18]

SELF-FOCUS MAKES YOU WEAK
IN THE FACE OF FAILURE

Far from making you come out on top, focusing on yourself can make you less resilient and weaker in the face of a challenge or failure. Though confidence and positive regard for yourself are of course good things, excessive self-esteem can be harmful because it usually entails comparing yourself to others.[19] Psychologists call this the "better than average effect": in general, most of us think of ourselves as being above average.[20]

Particularly in the United States, where individualism—being more focused on the self rather than identifying with a group—reigns, standing out is highly valued.[21] But it is impossible to always be above average and outperform others. At some point, you will fail. When your feelings of self-worth are dependent on your being successful in areas of your life that are important to you—for example, if you pride yourself on your professional accomplishments, your self-worth depends on your success at work—your self-esteem can crumble in the face of failure.[22] While having strong self-esteem has long been thought of as a good thing, it is the result rather than the cause of your achievements.[23] As such, inflated self-esteem can make you highly vulnerable if you do not do well facing life's inevitable challenges. If you are excessively self-focused, setbacks can cripple you.

SELF-FOCUS DAMAGES YOUR HEALTH
AND EMOTIONAL WELL-BEING

In addition to harming your professional career, self-focus negatively affects your physical and psychological health. A revealing series of studies showed that self-focus—measured by the frequency with which people used first-person singular pronouns (that is, *me, myself,* and *I*)—was related to higher blood pressure and increased coronary atherosclerosis, and predicted heart disease and mortality. The researchers found that in most cases these findings held up even when statistically controlling for traditional risk factors like smoking, cholesterol, and age.[24]

Psychologically, self-focus is strongly associated with negative emotions,[25] depression,[26] and particularly anxiety.[27] Rates of anxiety and depression correlate, in fact, with activity in the part of the brain responsible for thoughts about oneself.[28] Another psychological repercussion of self-focus is social isolation. After all, who wants to hang out with people who think about themselves all the time? Because it hurts your personal and professional relationships, self-focus leaves people depressed over the long run, according to Twenge.

In turn, the lack of social connection resulting from high self-focus can lead to severe health consequences. In 1988, James S. House, professor at the University of Michigan, conducted a landmark study looking at the impact of people's relationships on their health. He found that a lack of social relationships "constitute[s] a major risk factor for health—rivaling the effect of well-established health risk factors such as cigarette smoking, blood pressure, blood lipids, obesity and physical activity."[29]

What's more, according to House's and further studies, social isolation seems to accelerate the physiological decline of aging.[30] We tend to be aware of the basics of health: eat your veggies, go to the gym, and get proper rest. But we often overlook the importance of social connection—a feeling of positive connection with others. Loneliness has been linked to greater risk of disease, physiological aging, and earlier mortality. It has also been linked to the same cardiovascular risks associated with overuse of first-person singular pronouns (*me, myself,* and *I*). In fact, loneliness is even linked to increased inflammation at the cellular level and weakened immune response.[31] Finally, it harms your psychological well-being, increasing feelings of psychological distress.[32]

While self-focus is associated with poor outcomes on both personal and professional levels, focusing on other people—that is, other-focus, especially in the form of compassion—leads to tremendous benefits.

SUCCEEDING THROUGH COMPASSION

While the theory that you have to be self-focused to succeed actually hurts more than helps you, its opposite—the view that *to succeed, you need to be compassionate*—leads to positive results that are backed by science.

Compassion is the reverse of self-focus. In fact, it is profoundly other-focused. It involves empathically feeling someone else's pain and attempting to help that person in some way. Empathy is the emotional and physiological mechanism by which we understand someone else's emotion. It's the feeling that prompts us to say, "I *feel* your pain." Compassion is experiencing empathy for someone else's pain and having the desire to alleviate that pain. It involves sensitivity to the suffering of others and a desire to help them in a nonjudgmental way.[33]

Many people believe self-interest is innate, but research with infants and animals proves them wrong. These studies show that compassion is actually a natural instinct. Even rats are driven to empathize with a suffering rat and to go out of their way to help it out of its quandary.[34] Studies conducted at the prestigious Max Planck Institute in Germany suggest that compassion is an inborn trait in both humans and animals. A series of fascinating experiments showed that both chimpanzees and infants too young to have learned the rules of politeness spontaneously engaged in helpful behavior when confronted with another in need—even overcoming obstacles to do so.[35]

We often pride ourselves on our independence and on pulling ourselves up by our own bootstraps. Yet at the root of it, we are profoundly social creatures. Brené Brown, professor at the University of Houston Graduate College of Social Work, focuses her research on social connection. "A deep sense of love and belonging is an irresistible need of all people," she explains. "We are biologically, cognitively, physically, and spiritually wired to love, to be loved, and to belong. When those needs are not met, we don't function as we were meant to. We break. We fall apart. We numb. We ache. We hurt others. We get sick."[36] We may think we want money, power, fame, beauty, eternal youth, or a new car, but at the root of these desires is a need to belong, to be accepted, to connect with others.

Think of how painful it is to experience the opposite of compassion: loneliness or, worse, rejection—whether personal, professional, or romantic. Rejection leads to immense pain. Rejection is so unbearable that the same parts of the brain are activated during social rejection as during physical pain.[37] Stress due to conflict in relationships (work or otherwise) is so damaging that it causes increased inflammation levels in the body.[38] Both physically and psychologically, we experience compassionate social connection as wonderful, and rejection or loneliness as devastating.

Although we don't always prioritize compassion, we do intuitively realize that it leads to fulfillment. At Stanford, we conducted a study in which we asked five hundred people, "What brings you fulfillment?" Think for a few moments about how you might answer this question. We then reframed the question: "If you only had three days to live, what would you spend your time doing?" Think again about what you would respond before reading on.

You may have guessed it. At the top of both lists, the most popular responses were spending time with loved ones and helping people. Despite the fact that we may not live our lives that way, intuitively we know that our connections with others are the most meaningful elements of our lives.

Have you ever had a bad day when everything seemed to be going wrong, and then out of the blue you received a phone call from a friend or family member who desperately needed your help? All of a sudden, you were focused on that person's well-being. You were doing everything you could to help solve his or her problem. What happened to your terrible day? I've asked this question to many of my workshop participants, and they invariably give the same answer: their day turned around for the better. All of a sudden, they felt energized, alive, even happy. You go from being self-focused to taking care of another and from feeling down to being energized and positive.

Through compassion, you get in touch with your full potential for strength, power, and vitality. Through compassion, you find purpose.

When our brains move from a modality of self-focus and stress to a new modality of caring, nurturing, and connecting, our heart rate decelerates, vagal tone—our ability to relax and return to normal after stressful events—is strengthened, and we release hormones that are key for connection and bonding, such as oxytocin. In this new state, we feel at ease. Not only are we more compassionate to others, but we feel more deeply nurtured and positive on a personal level.

We all know how enjoyable it is to be on the receiving end of an act of kindness or generosity. But acting with compassion is as pleasurable as, if not more than, receiving something. That's the reason people go out of their way against their own self-interest to help others. It's why 25 percent of Americans volunteered their time for charitable causes in 2014 (a percentage that has remained consistent over the last years).[39] Or why Americans, on average, donate 3 percent of their yearly income, with middle- and lower-class individuals donating an even greater percentage.[40] Or why people pull over on the highway in the rain to help someone with a broken vehicle or to feed a stray cat.

A brain-imaging study[41] showed that the "pleasure centers" in the brain—the neural regions that are active when we experience pleasure—are equally active when we receive money ourselves as when we observe money going to charity. In another study,[42] participants received a sum of money and were instructed either to spend the money on themselves or to spend it on others. Those who spent money on others were happier. The research team also found that in children as young as two, giving treats to others increases happiness more than receiving treats.[43] The research team that conducted these studies found that these results stand up cross-culturally, regardless of whether countries are rich or poor. There is little doubt that we are wired for compassion—and it makes us happier and more fulfilled.

Since science shows that we are naturally wired to be other-focused and compassionate, why do we always hear that self-interest is the prime motivator? In large part because economists have propagated that notion. One study showed that students majoring in economics tend to act in a more self-interested way because they have been repeatedly exposed to this theory in their studies.[44] Another study suggests that people naturally have an inclination to help others but stop themselves because of the "norm of self-interest"—the theory that we all act selfishly. Why? Because they worry that others will believe they are helping out of self-interest and are therefore seeking something in return.

HOW COMPASSION LEADS TO SUCCESS

Drake is a happy, generous, and other-focused person. He is always interested in helping others whenever he can. He and his wife support a number of causes focused on improving the lives of children around the world who are at risk because of the poverty and violence that surround them. Kindness pervades his life.

So when Drake joined Bear Stearns, he was shocked by how the other managing directors mistreated the junior bankers—analysts, associates, and vice presidents. They had only their own best interest in mind and worked the junior staff into the ground—even abusively. For example, they would insist—after returning from a weekend in the Hamptons—that their staff go to work at 11 P.M. on Sunday evening and finish up a presentation or report by the next morning, even though it was not due to the client for days. The staff were then expected to work through the rest of the next day.

In addition to competing for bonuses and clients, the managing directors at Bear Stearns had to compete to get the firm's best junior bankers to join their projects. The junior bankers knew that their lives were going to be hellish no matter whom they worked for, so they tended to align themselves with managing directors who had a track record of earning the biggest deals so that they could get larger bonuses. When Drake first joined Bear Stearns, the junior bankers didn't know him and had no reason to join his team.

Drake was determined to stick to his values despite the self-interested culture that reigned. He treated the junior bankers with compassion and respect and gave them opportunities they would not have dreamed possible. For example, junior staff were seldom, if ever, invited to join a client meeting. Only vice presidents accompanied the managing directors. Drake, however, invited even the lowest-ranking among his staff and gave them important responsibilities.

For one deal, Drake had managed to attract just one analyst to work with him. He told her, "I think we have a high probability of winning this deal; I believe that just you and I can get this work done. It means you will have to perform the role of the analyst, associate, and vice president, and you will go pitch this IPO [initial public offering]. You will get a front-row seat to see what it's like to be a vice president on one of the hottest IPOs of the year." Not only did he invite the analyst (who would never otherwise have joined a client meeting), but he trained her and gave her the opportunity to present to the client. When this analyst later applied to business school, she did so with experience that far surpassed any of her fellow analysts.

When this turned out to be one of the best-performing IPOs of the year, and other junior bankers saw the experience this analyst earned, many sought to work for Drake. Here was someone who treated them with dignity, did not overwork them unnecessarily, cared for their professional development, and gave them unheard-of opportunities and experiences. Drake kept winning large deals, in part thanks to a loyal and hardworking team. Soon enough, the other managing directors started asking Drake, "What are you doing to get the good junior bankers to work with you?"

Drake put himself in the junior staff's shoes, understood their challenges and aspirations, and worked with them in a genuine desire to help them grow. As a consequence, he had positive, trusting, and caring interactions with others and built strong interpersonal bonds. Far more powerful and effective than self-interest, compassion helped Drake succeed and maintain his values even in a toxic environment.

As Drake's story shows and research substantiates, compassion is good for the bottom line, it's great for your relationships, and it inspires lasting loyalty. In addition, compassion significantly boosts your health.

COMPASSION IS GOOD FOR THE BOTTOM LINE

Kim Cameron[45] and his colleagues at the University of Michigan have studied the effect of compassionate practices in the workplace. Cameron defines these compassionate practices as

- caring for, being interested in, and maintaining responsibility for colleagues as friends;
- providing support for one another, including offering kindness and compassion when others are struggling;
- inspiring one another at work;
- emphasizing the meaningfulness of the work;
- avoiding blame and forgiving mistakes;
- treating one another with respect, gratitude, trust, and integrity.

In a research article published in the *Journal of Applied Behavioral Science,* Cameron explains that when organizations institute these practices, their performance levels dramatically improve: "They achieve significantly higher levels of organizational effectiveness—including financial performance, customer satisfaction, and productivity." He adds that the more compassionate the workplace, "the higher the performance in profitability, productivity, customer satisfaction, and employee engagement."

What is more, research shows that happier employees make for improved collegiality as well as a more congenial workplace.[46] Another large health-care study confirmed that a compassionate culture at work not only improved employee well-being and productivity but also improved *client* health outcomes and satisfaction.[47] In other words, compassion benefits you, your team, and your clients—bringing better results all around.

COMPASSION INCREASES YOUR STATUS
AND TRUSTWORTHINESS

To many people, the idea of applying compassion to a workplace seems foreign. After all, isn't it too touchy-feely? Won't it make you look soft? Actually, no, to the contrary. Research shows that rather than making you look soft, acts of kindness and altruism increase your status within a group.[48] Consider this choice: given two individuals with equivalent talent and skills, whom do you look up to and prefer to work with, promote, or invite onto a project? Undoubtedly the more compassionate one.

Wharton professor Adam Grant argues that kindness and compassion give us a far greater advantage than does self-focus. Nice guys do finish first, he explains, as long as they learn how not to let others take advantage of them. In his bestselling book, *Give and Take,* Grant explains that, yes, as many suspect, nice guys sometimes do lose out. People who care about others' well-being and look out for their colleagues and employees—the group Grant calls "givers"—are overrepresented at the bottom of the success ladder, having been mowed down by selfish "takers." But here's the surprising finding: Grant also reveals that "givers" are overrepresented at the very top of the success ladder. How can that be?

It turns out that givers are more liked and appreciated, and therefore become more influential. The difference between successful and unsuccessful givers often comes down to strategy: when givers learn strategies that prevent others from taking advantage of them, their "nice" qualities end up helping them succeed above and beyond anyone else. Why? In part because everyone loves working with them and appreciates them for their kind and giving qualities.

In addition to being pleasant and easy to work with, compassion makes you trustworthy. Trust is a crucial aspect of our lives because it makes us feel safe. Probably because managers and leaders determine our work experience—harsh and stressful or pleasant and enjoyable—we are especially sensitive to signs of trustworthiness in our leaders. Employees feel greater trust working with someone like Drake, who is kind. We prefer leaders who are warm rather than leaders who project tough characteristics Harvard professor Amy Cuddy has found.[49] Tough bosses, on the other hand, initiate a stress response in us. While our brains are attuned to threats (whether the threat is an angry lion or a raging boss), our brain's stress reactivity is significantly reduced when we observe kind behavior. As brain-imaging studies[50] show, when social relationships feel safe, the brain's stress response is attenuated.

In turn, trust increases a spirit of innovation. Grant told me that "when you respond in a frustrated, furious manner, the employee becomes less likely to take risks in the future because he or she worries about the negative consequences of making mistakes. In other words, you kill the culture of experimentation that is critical to learning and innovation." Grant refers to research led by Fiona Lee at the University of Michigan showing that promoting a culture of safety—rather than fear of negative consequences—helps encourage the spirit of experimentation so critical for creativity.[51]

Research shows that, for some, the idea of helping a person who is suffering or in need can feel daunting. One may feel overwhelmed by the situation and wish to get away from it. In her books and TED talk, Brené Brown[52] encapsulates this experience with one term: *vulnerability*. Being faced with another person's pain is difficult. Being compassionate toward that person may make you feel uncomfortable. It will require you to display deep authenticity, and we're not used to displaying vulnerability at work. Yet it's worth it.

Johann Berlin, CEO of the corporate well-being consulting company Transformational Leadership for Excellence,[53] shared with me[54] an experience he had while teaching a workshop in a Fortune 100 company. The participants were all from higher-level management. After an exercise in which pairs of participants shared an event from their lives with each other, one of the top executive managers approached Johann. Visibly moved by the experience, he said, "I've worked with my colleague for over twenty-five years and have never known about the difficult times in his life." In a short moment of authentic and vulnerable connection, this manager's compassion for and connection with his colleague deepened in ways it had not in decades of working together.

COMPASSION INSPIRES LOYALTY AND ENGAGEMENT

When we see someone engaging in a compassionate action or helping someone else, we get a warm-and-fuzzy, inspired feeling (you may even shed a tear or feel a chill). Psychologist Jonathan Haidt has appropriately named this state of being "elevation"—maybe because it makes you feel a little high for a moment.

In the workplace, elevation leads to increased loyalty. When Haidt and his colleagues applied his research on elevation to a business setting,[55] they found that when leaders treated their employees with fairness—that is, were polite, respectful, and sensitive—or were willing to sacrifice their leisure time, benefits, and career for the good of the organization or group, their employees experienced elevation. As a consequence, the employees felt more loyal and committed to their boss.

In addition, elevation seems to create a kinder culture around you. Haidt's data shows that when you experience elevation after watching someone help another, you're more likely to then do something kind for someone else. In the workplace, employees whose leader evoked elevation were then more likely to act in a helpful and friendly manner toward other employees, even when they had nothing to gain.

Another study showed that when leaders are fair, the members of their team display more collegial behavior and are more productive both individually and as a team.[56] In other words, compassionate behavior can create a more collaborative workplace environment. Researchers Nicholas Christakis and James Fowler have shown that if you are kind, those around you are more likely to act kindly. Research on "paying it forward" shows that when you work with people who help you, you will in turn be more likely to help others (and not necessarily just those who helped you).[57] In short, your compassionate behavior spreads around you, multiplying its benefits.

The story of Archana "Archie" Patchirajan,[58] an engineer from Bangalore—India's Silicon Valley—and the founder of an Internet startup, illustrates the impact of compassion on loyalty and collaboration. Archie, like Drake, does not operate from a place of self-focus. Her humility is perhaps her most disarming quality. She never describes her achievements, nor does she attempt to take the spotlight, but instead she listens attentively. She is extremely generous with advice; if she can help you, she will. When she is not working on engineering, she devotes countless hours to volunteering for several nonprofits. In brief, she is profoundly kind. To those who meet her, she is nothing short of inspiring.

Archie's beloved brother's dream was to found an Internet start-up. When he tragically died, Archie was determined to live out the dream in his honor. Like thousands of other hopeful start-up founders in Bangalore, she began working on a novel technology idea, hiring a team of engineers and slogging tirelessly toward her brother's dream.

Over time, however, the start-up began losing money, and sadly, Archie realized that she could no longer sustain the business. One day, she called her entire staff in for a meeting and announced that she had to let them go because the start-up was in dire straits and she could no longer pay them. A strange thing happened: her staff refused to leave. They stood by her side and declared that they would work for 50 percent of their pay rather than leave her. They worked so hard that a few years later Archie's company—Hubbl, which provides Internet advertising solutions—sold for 14 million dollars in the United States.

When I asked one of Archie's longest-standing employees what drove him to stay with her, these are some of the reasons he offered: "We all work as a family because Archie treats us as such." "Archie never fails to encourage us." "Archie knows everyone in the office and has a personal relationship with each one of us." "Archie does not get upset when we make mistakes but gives us the time to learn how to analyze and fix the situation." As evidenced by this employee's response, Archie's relationship with her employees is deeper than the usual employer-employee relationship. Why? She connects with them compassionately and as human beings first, employees second. She cares about them. As a consequence, they remain faithful to her through thick and thin and are highly engaged.

As Archie's story shows, if a manager is truly generous toward his or her employees, these employees are likely to follow suit, becoming more engaged and more loyal. In your own experience, you may have had a boss who inspired you because she was focused less on her own interests and more on yours. This person may have dedicated time and energy to your growth or learning with no benefit to herself. If that person were to call you today and ask for help, chances are that you would drop everything to do so. True loyalty comes from an interpersonal experience with someone who touched you—not just through a paycheck. Research shows that people prefer companionship and recognition over a large salary.[59]

Loyalty that can be bought is not true loyalty. Loyalty that comes from within—from a sense of inspiration and elevation—is much more powerful than loyalty that is easily swayed by a dollar figure. If you are a leader or colleague who really cares, people will be truly loyal to you. If your workers are loyal and engaged because you exhibit these qualities, they might not budge even if someone offered them more money.

COMPASSION IS GOOD FOR YOUR HEALTH

Unsurprisingly, increased trust and positive relationships generate health benefits. Unlike self-focus, compassionate and positive relationships with others are associated with

- 50 percent increased likelihood of longevity;[60]
- buffering against the health effects of stress;[61]
- a strengthened immune system;[62]
- reduced inflammation;[63]
- lower rates of anxiety and depression.[64]

Another reason compassion boosts our health is that it helps us recover more quickly in the face of life's stresses. A study conducted on over eight hundred people found that high levels of stress generally foretold earlier mortality—*except* in individuals who engaged in volunteer work.[65] In a long-term study with elderly couples, scientists compared individuals who spent time caring for others with those who had others care for them. The results showed that caring for others not only improved overall health but also lengthened lifespan.[66]

Whether compassion benefits health and emotional well-being, however, does depend on what motivates those acts of compassion. Individuals who engaged in volunteerism lived longer than their non-volunteering peers *only if* their reasons for volunteering were altruistic rather than self-serving. Exercising compassion and helping others must come from a genuine desire to do so and not be an act of self-interest.

STRENGTHENING YOUR COMPASSION MUSCLE

As I mentioned earlier, compassion involves putting yourself in other people's shoes, understanding the challenges they may be going through, and having an authentic desire to help them. The first step is empathy—putting yourself in others' shoes and really understanding how they are feeling. Drake understood the plight of his junior colleagues. He felt for them. Whether it's your boss's disappointment or your colleague's joy, being able to understand what other people are experiencing can help you interact with them in the most sensitive and appropriate way. As a consequence, they feel heard, understood, and respected; the relationship improves both personally and professionally.

If you tune into your body's automatic reaction to others, you will see that you naturally understand and respond to those around you. A close friend once walked into the room, and before I knew it, I heard myself exclaim, "What's wrong?!" I was surprised by my own words because I had not consciously registered that something was wrong. My friend wasn't crying or acting out of the ordinary, but I somehow knew without knowing. He asked for a hug and then told me one of his best friends had just been in a life-threatening accident and was badly wounded.

How had I known something was wrong? We all have a built-in empathy system that is extremely sensitive; it is faster and more automatic than our ability to reason—much like a reflex. We are like acute sounding boards or tuning forks. Even when we don't consciously know it, someone else's emotion or pain registers physiologically within us. We are wired for empathy. For example, another person's frown activates the frown muscles in our faces. In this way, we "read" other people's states of mind. This isn't superficial muscle mimicry, however; it is also psychological. Research[67] shows that seeing someone else's emotion activates the same neural circuits that are activated in our brains when we feel that emotion. Think of a time when a friend cried and you felt tears well up in your eyes. Or when she laughed and you fell into stitches too. Our empathy reflex is the reason we flinch when we see someone trip and fall, why a baby cries when hearing another cry, or why panic can spread in a crowd. It's the reason that the same regions of our brain are activated when we view someone else's pain as are activated when we experience pain ourselves.[68] It is the reason I knew something was wrong when my friend walked in the room, and surprised myself by asking the question before I had mentally registered that something appeared wrong.

How can you increase your compassion? Because we are wired for empathy, all we have to do is tap into this empathy reflex within us. Here are a couple of ways you can learn to do so.

Pay full attention when others are talking. When you talk to someone, listen and watch one hundred percent. A lot is communicated through facial expressions and even intonations. Listen to the other person's words, and notice how she expresses herself. Watch her facial expressions, particularly her eyes. The saying "Eyes are the windows to the soul" expresses a truth; research shows you can read people's emotions through their gaze.[69] One empathy research tool asks people to look at photographs of people's eyes only and to describe the emotion they see. The tilt of the face, the angle of an eyebrow, the creases at the side of the eye all reliably communicate emotion. By listening to and watching the other person, we can put ourselves in his shoes and respond appropriately or extend our support.

Verbalize the other person's point of view. Another way you can empathize with someone is to verbalize the emotion you observe they are feeling. Next time you are in a difficult conversation, try to acknowledge the other person's emotions. If you find a tactful way to show that you understand that your boss is upset ("It seems that you are very frustrated by [fill in the blank]") or that your colleague is sad ("You seem a little down today; please let me know if there is anything I can do to support you"), it may improve the relationship you have with the other person, who will feel heard and understood. Moreover, it will also ensure that you understand them correctly. Perhaps he isn't angry or sad but simply tired. If so, he can correct you, giving you a chance to understand what is going on.

Attend a compassion-training program. Much like a muscle or habit, compassion can be strengthened. Studies on compassion meditations—like loving-kindness meditation—or longer compassion-training programs, like the nine-session Compassion Cultivation Training program that we have offered through Stanford's Center for Compassion and Altruism Research and Education, have shown important benefits:

- They decrease stress hormones and inflammation, improving immune function and decreasing anxiety and depression.[70]

- They improve empathy. Participants who went through a compassion training were better able to recognize facial expressions of emotion[71] and showed changes in brain areas related to empathy, as my colleagues and I also found in other studies.[72]

- They make us kinder toward others and ourselves, and more willing to reach out and help others in need.[73]

- They strengthen people's ability to regulate their emotions and make them more resilient in the face of others' suffering.[74]

- They work quickly. While many compassion trainings are lengthy (nine sessions over nine weeks), my colleagues and I saw changes in feelings of in-the-moment social connection in as little as seven minutes of loving-kindness meditation.[75]

Whereas the self-focus myth we have been brought up to believe in actuality hampers our success and well-being, focusing on others through compassion produces extraordinary results. Research shows that when you live your life (be it at work or at home) from an authentic and caring place, you automatically breed trust around you. You inspire others and uplift them, and as a consequence they feel closer to you and even devoted to you. In addition to becoming more successful, you significantly boost your health and psychological well-being. Your impact spreads, as you create a culture of positivity that benefits those around you and reaps great results for you.

ACKNOWLEDGMENTS

For helping launch my writing career, a big thanks to Steve Kiesling—the first editor to accept an article pitch and a great mentor ever since! And a big hug to Daisy Grewal for encouraging me to start my column at *Psychology Today* way back when.

Thank you to Scott Kaufman for your kind e-mail suggesting I write a book, followed minutes later by a spontaneous introduction to my super-talented agent, Giles Anderson. Giles, thanks for your thoughtful and considered support and counsel throughout this process, as well as your great sense of humor.

Thanks to Genoveva Llosa for believing in me, inviting me to join HarperOne and providing wonderful edits. Thanks also to the excellent team at HarperOne: Hannah Rivera, Adia Colar, and Kim Dayman. I am deeply grateful for the opportunity to work with you all.

For fabulously insightful editing and comments on the manuscript, thank you to Rebecca McMillen, Peter Economy, Alison Peterson, Anett Gyurak, Dara Ghahremani, Sara Persson, Kate Northey, Carly Hamilton, Cassandra Long, and Jessica Waala.

A special thanks to all of my wonderful interviewees, who took the time to share their insights—thank you for inspiring me: Congressman Tim Ryan, Dr. James Doty, Brene Brown, Adam Grant, Elliot Berkman, Scott Barry Kaufman, Johann Berlin, Lolly Daskall, Archana Patchirajan, Jean Twenge, Jackie Rotman, Myron Scholes, Paul Gilbert, Adam Grant, Pico Iyer, Steve Porges, Kim Cameron,

Carole Pertofsky, Kristin Neff, Mike Heitmann, Sherron Lumley, Sarah Severn and Jake Dobberke.

To all my dear friends for their support and love throughout this process—especially my beloved Debanti, Uma, Johann, Dara, Maaheem, Kelly, Anett, Priya, Karishma, Carolan, Shubhu, Bill and Leslie.

Thank you to all my wonderful family members. In particular, thanks to my husband and my parents for their constant and unconditional love and support—not to mention their careful and lovingly detailed review of the manuscript. I have no words for how grateful I am for you every single day. I love you.

Finally, there are those very special men and women who, throughout time, have worked tirelessly to bring light, knowledge, and compassion to the world—wisdom that has been passed on through the ages to this day. Sri Sri Ravi Shankar has especially graced my life, touched my heart, and inspired my thinking.

NOTES

INTRODUCTION

1. "Regus-Commissioned Survey Reveals Stress Levels Rising Among US Workers," Regus Group, http://www.prnewswire.com/news-releases/regus-commissioned-survey-reveals-stress-levels-rising-among-us-workers-71658307.html.

2. "Facts & Statistics," Anxiety and Depression Association of America, http://www.adaa.org/about-adaa/press-room/facts-statistics.

3. L. A. Pratt et al., "Antidepressant Use in Persons Aged 12 and Over: United States, 2005–2008," NCHS data brief no. 76 (Hyattsville, MD: National Center for Health Statistics, 2011), http://www.cdc.gov/nchs/data/databriefs/db76.htm.

4. "Report: State of the American Workplace," Gallup, September 22, 2014, http://www.gallup.com/services/176708/state-american-workplace.aspx.

5. Barbara L. Fredrickson, "What Good Are Positive Emotions?" *Review of General Psychology* 2, no. 3 (1998): 300–19, http://www.unc.edu/peplab/publications/Fredrickson%201998.pdf.

6. K. Subramaniam et al., "A Brain Mechanism for Facilitation of Insight by Positive Affect," *Journal of Cognitive Neuroscience* 21 (2009): 415–32.

7. Andrew J. Oswald, "Happiness and Productivity," *Journal of Organizational Behavior* 20 (2009): 25–30, http://www2.warwick.ac.uk/fac/soc/economics/staff/eproto/workingpapers/happinessproductivity.pdf.

8. M. Tugade and B. Fredrickson, "Resilient Individuals Use Positive Emotions to Bounce Back from Negative Emotional Experiences," *Journal of Personality and Social Psychology* 86 (2011): 320–33.

9. E. J. Boothby et al., "Shared Experiences Are Amplified," *Psychological Science* 25, no. 12 (2014): 2209–16, DOI: 10.1177/0956797614551162.

10. Alan W. Gray et al., "Laughter's Influence on the Intimacy of Self-Disclosure," *Human Nature* 26, no. 1 (2015): 28–43, DOI: 10.1007 /s12110-015-9225-8.

11. J. E. Dutton et al., "Pathways for Positive Identity Construction at Work: Four Types of Positive Identity and the Building of Social Resources," *Academy of Management Review* 35 (2010): 265–93.

12. J. M. Lilius et al., "The Contours and Consequences of Compassion at Work," *Journal of Organizational Behavior* 29 (2008): 193–218, DOI: 10.1002/job.508.

13. J. M. Kanov, "Compassion in Organizational Life," *American Behavioral Scientist* 47 (2004): 808–27, DOI: 10.1177/0002764203260211.

14. J. M. Lilius et al., "Compassion Revealed: What We Know About Compassion at Work (and Where We Need to Know More)," in *The Handbook of Positive Organizational Scholarship*, ed. K. Cameron and G. Spreitzer (Oxford: Oxford University Press, 2011), 273–87.

15. A. Bakker, "An Evidence-Based Model of Work Engagement," *Current Directions in Psychological Science* 20 (2011): 265–69, DOI: 10.1177/0963721411414534.

16. S. G. Barsade and D. E. Gibson, "Why Does Affect Matter in Organizations?" *Academy of Management Perspectives* 21 (2007): 36–59.

17. Nilly Mor and Jennifer Winquist, "Self-Focused Attention and Negative Affect: A Meta-analysis," *Psychological Bulletin* 128, no. 4 (2002): 638–62, http://psycnet.apa.org/journals/bul/128/4/638/.

18. B. Fredrickson et al., "Open Hearts Build Lives: Positive Emotions, Induced Through Loving-Kindness Meditation, Build Consequential Personal Resources," *Journal of Personality and Social Psychology* 95 (2011): 1045–62, DOI: 10.1037/a0013262.

19. J. H. Fowler and N. A. Christakis, "Dynamic Spread of Happiness in a Large Social Network: Longitudinal Analysis over 20 Years in the Framingham Heart Study," *British Medical Journal* 337 (2008): 1–9, DOI: http://dx.doi.org/10.1136/bmj.a2338.

20. Jennifer E. Stellar et al., "Positive Affect and Markers of Inflammation: Discrete Positive Emotions Predict Lower Levels of Inflammatory Cytokines," *Emotion* 15, no. 2 (2015): 129–33, DOI: 10.1037/emo 0000033; and Lee S. Berk and Stanley Tan, "Mirthful Laughter, as Adjunct Therapy in Diabetic Care, Increases HDL Cholesterol and Attenuates Inflammatory Cytokines and C-RP and Possible CVD Risk," *FASEB Journal,* Supplement 990.1 (2009), http://www.fasebj.org/cgi /content/meeting_abstract/23/1_MeetingAbstracts/990.1.

21. B. Fredrickson and R. Levenson, "Positive Emotions Speed Recovery from the Cardiovascular Sequelae of Negative Emotions," *Cognition and Emotion* 12 (1998): 191–220; and B. Fredrickson et al., "The Undoing Effects of Positive Emotions," *Motivation and Emotion* 24 (2000): 237–58.

22. "Fight Memory Loss with a Smile (or Chuckle)," *Science Daily*, April 27, 2014, http://www.sciencedaily.com/releases/2014/04/140427185149 .htm; and Lee S. Berk and Stanley A. Tan, "[Beta]-Endorphin and HGH Increase Are Associated with Both the Anticipation and Experience of Mirthful Laughter," *FASEB Journal,* Supplement A382 (2006), http://www.fasebj.org/cgi/content/meeting_abstract/20/4/A382-b.

CHAPTER 1: STOP CHASING THE FUTURE

1. Alan Watts, *The Book: On the Taboo Against Knowing Who You Are* (Knopf Doubleday Publishing, Random House Bertelsmann), 112.

2. Interview with Jackie Rotman, June 5, 2015.

3. Interview with Carole Pertofsky, June 5, 2015.

4. Walter Mischel et al., "Cognitive and Attentional Mechanisms in Delay of Gratification," *Journal of Personality and Social Psychology* 21, no. 2 (1972): 204–18, DOI: 10.1037/h0032198.

5. Martin E. P. Seligman, *Authentic Happiness: Using the New Positive Psychology to Realize Your Potential for Lasting Fulfillment* (New York: Simon & Schuster, 2002), 120.

6. Michael T. Treadway et al., "Dopaminergic Mechanisms of Individual Differences in Human Effort-Based Decision-Making," *Journal of Neuroscience* 32, no. 18 (2012): 6170–76, DOI: 10.1523/JNEUROSCI .6459-11.2012.

7. M. D. Griffiths, "Workaholism Is Still a Useful Construct," *Addiction Research and Theory* 3 (2005): 97–100.

8. Leslie A. Perlow, "Overcome Your Work Addiction," *Harvard Business Review,* May 2, 2012, https://hbr.org/2012/05/overcome-your-work-addiction.html.

9. T. D. Wilson and D. T. Gilbert, "Affective Forecasting: Knowing What We Want," *Current Directions in Psychological Science* 14 (2005): 131–34, DOI: 10.1111/j.0963-7214.2005.00355.x.

10. Philip Brickman et al., "Lottery Winners and Accident Victims: Is Happiness Relative?" *Journal of Personality and Social Psychology* 36, no. 8 (1978): 917–27, http://psycnet.apa.org/journals/psp/36/8/917/.

11. Jean-Louis van Gelder et al., "Vividness of the Future Self Predicts Delinquency," *Psychological Science* 24, no. 6 (2013): 974–80, http://www.anderson.ucla.edu/faculty/hal.hershfield/resources/Research/VanGelderHershfieldNordgren_VividnessOfFutureSelfDelinquencyRevision.pdf.

12. Hal Ersner-Hershfield et al., "Don't Stop Thinking About Tomorrow: Individual Differences in Future Self-Continuity Account for Saving," *Judgment and Decision Making* 4, no. 4 (2009): 280–86, http://www.anderson.ucla.edu/faculty/hal.hershfield/resources/Research/2009-Ersner-Hershfield.pdf.

13. Malissa A. Clark and Boris Baltes, "All Work and No Play? A Meta-analytic Examination of the Correlates and Outcomes of Workaholism," *Journal of Management* (2014), advance online publication, DOI: 10.1177/0149206314522301.

14. Clark and Baltes, "All Work and No Play?"

15. George Halkos and Dimitrios Bousinakis, "The Effect of Stress and Satisfaction on Productivity," *International Journal of Productivity and*

Performance Management 59, no. 5 (2010): 415–31, http://www.emerald insight.com/doi/abs/10.1108/17410401011052869.

16. J. Smallwood et al., "Shifting Moods Wandering Minds: Negative Moods Lead the Mind to Wander," *Emotion* 9 (2009): 271–76.

17. Clark and Baltes, "All Work and No Play?"

18. Clark and Baltes, "All Work and No Play?"

19. Helene Hembrooke and Geri Gay, "The Laptop and the Lecture: The Effects of Multitasking in Learning Environments," *Journal of Computing in Higher Education* 15, no. 1 (2003): 46–64, http://link.springer .com/article/10.1007/BF02940852#page-1.

20. E. Ophir et al., "Cognitive Control in Media Multitaskers," *Proceedings of the National Academy of Sciences* 106 (2009): 15583–87, DOI: 10.1073/pnas.0903620106.

21. Marcel Adam Just et al., "A Decrease in Brain Activation Associated with Driving When Listening to Someone Speak," *Brain Research* 1205 (2008): 70–80, DOI: 10.1016/j.brainres.2007.12.075.

22. Mark W. Becker et al. "Media Multitasking Is Associated with Symptoms of Depression and Social Anxiety," *Cyberpsychology, Behavior, and Social Networking* 16, no. 2 (2013): 132–35

23. Mihály Csíkszentmihályi et al., "Flow," in *Flow and the Foundations of Positive Psychology* (Dordrecht: Springer Netherlands, 2014), 227–38.

24. Csíkszentmihályi et al., "Flow," 227–38.

25. Matthew A. Killingsworth and Daniel T. Gilbert, "A Wandering Mind Is an Unhappy Mind," *Science* 330, no. 6006 (2010): 932, DOI: 10.1126/science.1192439.

26. Michael S. Franklin et al., "The Silver Lining of a Mind in the Clouds: Interesting Musings Are Associated with Positive Mood While Mind-Wandering," *Frontiers in Psychology* 4 (2013): 583, DOI: 10.3389 /fpsyg.2013.00583.

27. Franklin et al., "Silver Lining," 583.

28. Andrew K. Przybylski, "Can You Connect with Me Now? How the Presence of Mobile Communication Technology Influences Face-to-

Face Conversation Quality," *Journal of Social and Personal Relationships* (2012), advance online publication, DOI: 10.1177/0265407512453827.

29. Robert J. House et al., "Personality and Charisma in the U.S. Presidency: A Psychological Theory of Leader Effectiveness," *Administrative Science Quarterly* 36, no. 3 (1991): 364–96, DOI: 10.2307/2393201.

30. Reinhard Bendix, *Max Weber: An Intellectual Portrait* (New York: Anchor Books, 1962), 88.

31. Kenneth J. Levine et al., "Measuring Transformational and Charismatic Leadership: Why Isn't Charisma Measured?" *Communication Monographs* 77, no. 4 (2010): 576–91, DOI: 10.1080/03637751.2010.499368.

32. E. D. Wesselmann et al., "To Be Looked at as Though Air: Civil Attention Matters," *Psychological Science* 23, no. 2 (2012): 166–68, DOI: 10.1177/0956797611427921.

33. M. Corbetta et al., "A Common Network of Functional Areas for Attention and Eye Movements," *Neuron* 21, no. 4 (1998): 761–73.

34. Ronald S. Burt, "Network Brokerage: How the Social Network Around You Creates Competitive Advantage for Innovation and Top-Line Growth," handout, Strategic Leadership in Management Networks from Chicago Booth, Chicago, IL, 2015, http://faculty .chicagobooth.edu/ronald.burt/teaching/pdfs/1brokerage.pdf.

35. Meliksah Demir et al., "Looking to Happy Tomorrows with Friends: Best and Close Friendships as They Predict Happiness," *Journal of Happiness Studies* 8, no. 2 (2007): 243–71, http://link.springer.com /article/10.1007/s10902-006-9025-2#page-1.

36. "Most Used Mind & Body Practices," National Center for Complementary and Integrative Health, https://nccih.nih.gov/research /statistics/NHIS/2012/mind-body/meditation.

37. Judson Brewer et al., "Meditation Experience Is Associated with Differences in Default Mode Network Activity and Connectivity," *Proceedings of the National Academy of Sciences* 108, no. 50 (2011): 20254–259.

38. Annetrin Jytte Basler, "Pilot Study Investigating the Effects of Ayurvedic *Abhyanga* Massage on Subjective Stress Experience," *Journal*

of Alternative and Complementary Medicine 17, no. 5 (2011): 435–40, DOI: 10.1089/acm.2010.0281.

39. Daniel B. Levinson et al., "A Mind You Can Count On: Validating Breath Counting as a Behavioral Measure of Mindfulness," *Frontiers in Psychology* 5 (2014): 1202, DOI: 10.3389/fpsyg.2014.01202.

40. Fred B. Bryant, "A Four-Factor Model of Perceived Control: Avoiding, Coping, Obtaining, and Savoring," *Journal of Personality* 57, no. 4 (1989): 773–97, DOI: 10.1111/j.1467-6494.1989.tb00494.x.

41. Nick Bilton, "How to Take a Break from Your Technology," Bits, *New York Times,* May 13, 2013, http://bits.blogs.nytimes.com/2013/05/13/how-to-take-a-break-from-your-technology/?_r=0.

42. Timothy D. Wilson et al., "Just Think: The Challenges of the Disengaged Mind," *Science* 345, no. 6192 (2014): 75–77, DOI: 10.1126/science.1250830.

CHAPTER 2: STEP OUT OF OVERDRIVE

1. Michael Seamark, "Lloyds Boss Goes Sick with 'Stress': Shock Departure Eight Months into Job," *Daily Mail,* November 2011, http://www.dailymail.co.uk/news/article-2056474/Lloyds-CEO-Antonio-Horta-Osorio-takes-medical-leave.html.

2. "Definitions," American Psychological Association and American Institute of Stress, http://www.stress.org/daily-life/.

3. Jill Treanor, "Lloyds Chief 'Did Not Sleep for Five Days,' " *Guardian,* December 15, 2011, http://www.theguardian.com/business/2011/dec/15/lloyds-chief-horta-osorio-sleeping-problems.

4. J. L. Tsai et al., "Cultural Variation in Affect Valuation," *Journal of Personality and Social Psychology* 90 (2006): 288–307, DOI: 10.1037/0022-3514.90.2.288; and J. L. Tsai et al., "Influence and Adjustment Goals: Sources of Cultural Differences in Ideal Affect," *Journal of Personality and Social Psychology* 92 (2007): 1102–17, DOI: 10.1037/0022-3514.92.6.1102.

5. Roman Duncko et al., "Acute Exposure to Stress Improves Performance in Trace Eyeblink Conditioning and Spatial Learning Tasks

in Healthy Men," *Learning and Memory* 14, no. 5 (2007): 329–35, DOI: 10.1101/lm.483807.

6. Firdaus Dhabhar et al., "Short-Term Stress Enhances Cellular Immunity and Increases Early Resistance to Squamous Cell Carcinoma," *Brain Behavior and Immunity* 24, no. 1 (2010): 127–37, DOI: 10.1016/j.bbi.2009.09.004; F. S. Dhabhar, "Psychological Stress and Immunoprotection Versus Immunopathology in the Skin," *Clinics in Dermatology* 31, no. 1, (2013): 18–30, DOI:10.1016/j.clindermatol .2011.11.003; F. S. Dhabhar et al., "Effects of Stress on Immune Cell Distribution—Dynamics and Hormonal Mechanisms," *Journal of Immunology* 154 (1995): 5511–27; and Dhabhar and B. S. McEwen, "Stress-Induced Enhancement of Antigen-Specific Cell-Mediated Immunity," *Journal of Immunology* 156 (1996): 2608–15.

7. F. S. Dhabhar, "Enhancing Versus Suppressive Effects of Stress on Immune Function: Implications for Immunoprotection and Immunopathology," *Neuroimmunomodulation* 16 (2009): 300–17; and F. S. Dhabhar, "Effects of Stress on Immune Function: The Good, the Bad, and the Beautiful," *Immunologic Research* 58 (2014): 193–210.

8. F. S. Dhabhar and B. S. McEwen, "Acute Stress Enhances While Chronic Stress Suppresses Immune Function in Vivo: A Potential Role for Leukocyte Trafficking," *Brain Behavior & Immunity* 11 (1997): 286–306.

9. P. H. Rosenberger et al., "Surgery Stress Induced Immune Cell Redistribution Profiles Predict Short- and Long-Term Postsurgical Recovery: A Prospective Study," *Journal of Bone and Joint Surgery* 91 (2009): 2783–94.

10. F. S. Dhabhar et al., "Stress-Induced Redistribution of Immune Cells—From Barracks to Boulevards to Battlefields: A Tale of Three Hormones," *Psychoneuroendocrinology* 37 (2012): 1345–68.

11. D. Kaufer et al., "Acute Stress Facilitates Long-Lasting Changes in Cholinergic Gene Expression," *Nature* 393 (1998): 373–77, DOI: 10.1038/30741; and Roman Duncko, "Acute Exposure to Stress Improves Performance in Trace Eyeblink Conditioning and Spatial

Learning Tasks in Healthy Men," *Learning & Memory* 14 (2007): 329–35, DOI: 10.1101/lm.483807.

12. R. M. Yerkes and J. D. Dodson, "The Relation of Strength of Stimulus to Rapidity of Habit-Formation," *Journal of Comparative Neurology and Psychology* 18 (1908): 459–82, DOI: 10.1002/cne.920180503.

13. B. von Dawans et al., "The Social Dimension of Stress Reactivity: Acute Stress Increases Prosocial Behavior in Humans," *Psychological Science* 23 (2012): 651–60, DOI: 10.1177/0956797611431576.

14. Neil Schneiderman et al., "Stress and Health: Psychological, Behavioral, and Biological Determinants," *Annual Review of Clinical Psychology* 1 (2005): 607, DOI: 10.1146/annurev.clinpsy.1.102803.144141.

15. G. E. Miller et al., "Psychological Stress and Antibody Response to Influenza Vaccination: When Is the Critical Period for Stress, and How Does It Get Inside the Body?" *Psychosomatic Medicine* 66 (2004): 207–14, http://www.psy.cmu.edu/~scohen/fluvacc04.pdf.

16. Sheldon Cohen et al., "Chronic Stress, Glucocorticoid Receptor Resistance, Inflammation, and Disease Risk," *Proceedings of the National Academy of Sciences* 109 (2012): 5995–99, DOI: 10.1073/pnas.1118355109.

17. E. S. Epel et al., "Accelerated Telomere Shortening in Response to Life Stress," *Proceedings of the National Academy of Sciences* 101, no. 49 (2004): 17312–15, DOI: 10.1073/pnas.0407162101.

18. C. Kirschbaum et al., "Stress and Treatment Induced Elevations of Cortisol Levels Associated with Impaired Declarative Memory in Healthy Adults," *Life Sciences* 58, no. 17 (1996): 1475–83; David M. Diamond et al., "Psychological Stress Impairs Spatial Working Memory: Relevance to Electrophysiological Studies of Hippocampal Function," *Behavioral Neuroscience* 110, no. 4 (1996): 661–72, DOI: 10.1037//0735-7044.110.4.661; and N. Y. Oie et al., "Psychosocial Stress Impairs Working Memory at High Loads: An Association with Cortisol Levels and Memory Retrieval," *Stress* 9, no. 3 (2006): 133–41, DOI: 10.1080/10253890600965773. See also http://informahealthcare.com/doi/abs/10.1080/10253890600965773.

19. J. Shanteau and G. A. Dino, "Environmental Stressor Effects on Creativity and Decision Making," in *Time Pressure and* Stress *in Human Judgment and Decision Making*, ed. O. Svenson and A. J. Maule (New York: Plenum, 1993): 293–308, DOI: 10.1007/9781475768466; and K. Byron et al., "The Relationship Between Stressors and Creativity: A Meta-Analysis Examining Competing Theoretical Models," *Journal of Applied Psychology* 95 (2010): 201–12.

20. L. Mujica-Parodi et al., "Chemosensory Cues to Conspecific Emotional Stress Activate the Amygdala in Humans," *PLoS One* 4, no. 7 (2009), DOI: 10.1371/journal.pone.0006415.

21. Roy F. Baumeister et al., "Bad Is Stronger Than Good," *Review of General Psychology* 5, no. 4 (2001): 323–70, DOI: 10.1037//1089-2680.5.4.323; and S. Gable and J. Haidt, "What (And Why) Is Positive Psychology," *Review of General Psychology* 9 (2005): 103–10.

22. Interview with Paul Gilbert, January 29, 2014.

23. K. Kushlev and E. W. Dunn, "Checking E-mail Less Frequently Reduces Stress," *Computers in Human Behavior* 43 (2015), 1458–66, DOI: 10.1016/j.chb.2014.11.005.

24. Gloria J. Mark and Stephen Voida, "A Pace Not Dictated by Electrons": An Empirical Study of Work Without E-mail," in *Proceeding of the Thirtieth Annual SIGCHI Conference on Human Factors in Computing Systems (CHI'12)* (New York: ACM Press, 2012), 555–64, DOI: 10.1145/2207676.2207754.

25. Sara Radicati, ed., "E-mail Statistics Report, 2011–2015," Radicati Group, May 2011, http://www.radicati.com/wp/wp-content/uploads/2011/05/E-mail-Statistics-Report-2011-2015-Executive-Summary.pdf.; and Sara Radicati, ed., "E-mail Statistics Report, 2014–2015," Radicati Group, April 2014, http http://www.radicati.com/wp/wp-content/uploads/2014/01/Email-Statistics-Report-2014-2018-Executive-Summary.pdf.

26. Baumeister et al., "Bad Is Stronger Than Good"; and Gable and Haidt, "Positive Psychology."

27. Baumeister et al., "Bad Is Stronger Than Good"; and Gable and Haidt, "Positive Psychology."

28. Alan Schwarz, "Workers Seeking Productivity in a Pill Are Abusing A.D.H.D. Drugs," *New York Times,* April 18, 2015, http://www.nytimes.com/2015/04/19/us/workers-seeking-productivity-in-a-pill-are-abusing-adhd-drugs.html?_r=0.

29. D. M. Wegner, "Ironic Processes of Mental Control," *Psychological Review* 101 (1994): 34–52, http://dx.doi.org/10.1037/0033-295X.101.1.34.

30. J. J. Gross, "Emotion Regulation: Affective, Cognitive, and Social Consequences," *Psychophysiology* 39, no. 3 (2002): 281–91, DOI: 10.1017.S0048577201393198.

31. E. A. Butler et al., "The Social Consequences of Expressive Suppression," *Emotion* 3, no. 1 (2003): 48–67, DOI: 10.1037/1528-3542.3.1.48.

32. Thync: http://www.thync.com/.

33. Sri Sri Ravi Shankar, "5 Steps to Healthier Living," *Huffington Post,* http://www.huffingtonpost.com/sri-sri-ravi-shankar/healthier-living-new-year_b_1130296.html.

34. P. Philippot and S. Blairy, "Respiratory Feedback in the Generation of Emotion," *Cognition and Emotion* 16, no. 5 (2002): 605–27, DOI: 10.1080/02699930143000392.

35. Philippot and Blairy, "Respiratory Feedback," 605–27.

36. Jordan Etkin et al., "Pressed for Time? Goal Conflict Shapes How Time Is Perceived, Spent, and Valued," *Journal of Marketing Research* 52, no. 3 (2015): 394–406, DOI: 10.1509/jmr.14.0130.

37. E. M. Seppälä et al., "Breathing-Based Meditation Decreases Posttraumatic Stress Disorder Symptoms in U.S. Military Veterans: A Randomized Controlled Longitudinal Study," *Journal of Traumatic Stress* 27, no. 4 (2014): 397–405, DOI: 10.1002/jts.21936.

38. "Yoga for Anxiety and Depression," *Harvard Health Publications,* April 1, 2009 http://www.health.harvard.edu/mind-and-mood/yoga-for-anxiety-and-depression.

39. The program for veterans was offered by Project Welcome Home Troops, a project of the International Association for Human Values. Similar workshops are offered for community members through the Art of Living Foundation.

40. Interview with Stephen Porges, January 29, 2014.

41. A. Kogan et al., "Vagal Activity Is Quadratically Related to Prosocial Traits, Prosocial Emotions, and Observer Perceptions of Prosociality," *Journal of Personality and Social Psychology* 107, no. 6 (2014), DOI: 10.1037/a0037509; and Philippot and Blairy, "Respiratory Feedback," 605–27.

42. E. A. Wehrwein et al., "A Single, Acute Bout of Yogic Breathing Reduces Arterial Catecholamines and Cortisol," *Journal of the Federation of American Societies for Experimental Biology,* Supplement 893.16 (2012); N. Janakiramaiah et al., "Therapeutic Efficacy of Sudarshan Kriya Yoga (SKY) in Dysthymic Disorder," *National Institute for Mental Health and Neuro Sciences Journal* 17 (1998): 21–28; and A. Vedamurthachar et al., "Antidepressant Efficacy and Hormonal Effects of Sudarshana Kriya Yoga (SKY) in Alcohol Dependent Individuals," *Journal of Affective Disorders* 94 (2006): 249–53.

43. D. J. Plews et al., "Training Adaptation and Heart Rate Variability in Elite Endurance Athletes: Opening the Door to Effective Monitoring," *Sports Med* 43, no. 9 (2013): 773–81, DOI: 10.1007/s40279-013 -0071-8.

44. G. N. Bratman et al., "The Benefits of Nature Experience: Improved Affect and Cognition," *Landscape and Urban Planning* 138 (2014): 41–50, DOI: 10.1016/j.landurbplan.2015.02.005.

45. Kate E. Lee et al., "40-Second Green Roof Views Sustain Attention: The Role of Micro-Breaks in Attention Restoration," *Journal of Environmental Psychology* 42 (2015): 182–89.

46. Melanie Rudd et al., "Awe Expands People's Perception of Time, Alters Decision Making, and Enhances Well-Being," *Psychological Science* 23, no. 10 (2012): 1130–36.

47. S. Cohen et al., "Does Hugging Provide Stress-Buffering Social Support? A Study of Susceptibility to Upper Respiratory Infection and Illness," *Psychological Science* 26, no. 2 (2015): 135–47, DOI: 10.1177/0956797614559284.

48. Jeff Dominic, "Lloyds Comeback Kid Antonio Horta-Osorio Halts Rot," *Scotsman*, May 11, 2014, http://www.scotsman.com/business /management/lloyds-comeback-kid-antonio-horta-osorio-halts-rot-1 -3406148.

CHAPTER 3: MANAGE YOUR ENERGY

1. Tony Schwartz and Jim Loehr, *The Power of Full Engagement: Managing Energy, Not Time, Is the Key to High Performance and Personal Renewal* (New York: Simon & Schuster), 17.

2. Mike Hodges, "The 10 Most Influential Figures in MMA," *Bleacher Report*, July 19, 2010, http://bleacherreport.com/articles/422132 -top-10-influential-figures-in-mma/page/11.

3. Interview with Mike Heitmann, November 29, 2014.

4. C. Maslach, Burnout: A Social Psychological Analysis, in J. W. Jones, ed., *The Professional Burnout: Recent Developments in Theory and Research* (New York: Hemisphere, 1993), 20.

5. S. Jackson et al., "Toward an Understanding of the Burnout Phenomenon," *Journal of Applied Psychology* 71, no. 4 (1986): 630–40.

6. "Prevalence of Burnout, Depression, and Suicidal Ideation Among U.S. Physicians as of 2012," Statista, http://www.statista.com/statistics /316027/burnout-depression-and-suicidal-ideation-in-us-physicians/.

7. "Percentage of Total Burned Out Financial Professionals in Selected Countries in 2014, by Gender," Statista, http://www.statista.com /statistics/316061/total-burnout-in-financial-professionals-by-country -and-gender/.

8. Caroline Preston, "Burnout, Low Pay May Drive Young Charity Workers Away, Survey Finds," *Chronicle of Philanthropy*, March 22,

2007, https://philanthropy.com/article/Burnout-Low-Pay-May
-Drive/178465.

9. Mayo Clinic Staff, "Job Burnout: How to Spot It and Take Action," Mayo Clinic, December 8, 2012, http://www.mayoclinic.org /healthy-lifestyle/adult-health/in-depth/burnout/art-20046642.

10. Stephen E. Humphrey et al., "Integrating Motivational, Social, and Contextual Work Design Features: A Meta-Analytic Summary and Theoretical Extension of the Work Design Literature," *Journal of Applied Psychology* 92, no. 5 (2007): 1332–56, http://psycnet.apa.org /journals/apl/92/5/1332/.

11. Interview with Elliot Berkman, March 17, 2015.

12. Jeanne L. Tsai et al., "Cultural Variation in Affect Valuation," *Journal of Personality and Social Psychology* 90, no. 2 (2006): 288–307, http:// psycnet.apa.org/journals/psp/90/2/288/.

13. Jeanne L. Tsai et al., "Influence and Adjustment Goals: Sources of Cultural Differences in Ideal Affect," *Journal of Personality and Social Psychology* 92, no. 6 (2007): 1100–17, DOI: 10.1037/0022-3514.92.6.1102.

14. Charlotte Vanoyen Witvliet and Scott R. Vrana, "Psychophysiological Responses as Indices of Affective Dimensions," *Psychophysiology* 32, no. 5 (1995): 436–43, DOI: 10.1111/j.1469-8986.1995.tb02094.x.

15. Kevin N. Ochsner et al., "Rethinking Feelings: An fMRI Study of the Cognitive Regulation of Emotion," *Journal of Cognitive Neuroscience* 14, no. 8 (2002): 1215–29, http://brainimaging.waisman.wisc .edu/~perlman/0903-EmoPaper/CogRegEmoOschner.2002.pdf.

16. Oscar Wilde, *I Can Resist Everything Except Temptation, and Other Quotations from Oscar Wilde*, ed. Karl Beckson (New York: Columbia University Press, 1997).

17. Nansook Park et al., "Character Strengths in Fifty-Four Nations and the Fifty US States," *Journal of Positive Psychology* 1, no. 3 (2006): 118–29, DOI: 10.1080/17439760600619567.

18. Kelly A. Snyder et al., "What Form of Memory Underlies Novelty Preferences?" *Psychonomic Bulletin & Review* 15, no. 2 (2008): 315–21, DOI: 10.3758/PBR.15.2.315.

19. D. M. Wegner, "Ironic Processes of Mental Control," *Psychological Review* 101 (1994): 34–52, http://dx.doi.org/10.1037/0033-295X.101.1.34.

20. R. F. Baumeister et al., "The Strength Model of Self-Control," *Current Directions in Psychological Science* 16, no. 6 (2007): 351–55.

21. R. F. Baumeister et al., "Ego Depletion: Is the Active Self a Limited Resource?," *Journal of Personality and Social Psychology* 74 (1998): 1252–65.

22. Baumeister et al., "Ego Depletion," 1252–65.

23. M. S. Hagger et al., "Ego Depletion and the Strength Model of Self-Control: A Meta-Analysis," *Psychological Bulletin* 136, no. 4 (2010): 495–525, DOI: 10.1037/a0019486.

24. Martin S. Hagger and Nikos L. D. Chatzisarantis, "A Multi-Lab Pre-Registered Replication of the Ego-Depletion Effect," *Psychological Science* (In Press).

25. Mark Muraven et al., "Daily Fluctuations in Self-Control Demands and Alcohol Intake," *Psychology of Addictive Behaviors* 19, no. 2 (2005): 140–47, DOI: 10.1037/0893-164X.19.2.140.

26. Matthew T. Gailliot and Roy F. Baumeister, "The Physiology of Willpower: Linking Blood Glucose to Self-Control," *Personality and Social Psychology Review* 11, no. 4 (2007): 303–27, DOI: 10.1177/1088868307303030.

27. Maryam Kouchaki and Isaac H. Smith, "The Morning Morality Effect: The Influence of Time of Day on Unethical Behavior," *Psychological Science* 25, no. 1 (2014): 95–102, DOI: 10.1177/0956797613498099.

28. F. Gino et al., "Unable to Resist Temptation: How Self-Control Depletion Promotes Unethical Behavior," *Organizational Behavior and Human Decision Processes* 115, no. 2 (2011): 191–203.

29. M. Gailliot et al., "Self-Control Relies on Glucose as a Limited Energy Source: Willpower Is More Than a Metaphor," *Journal of Personality and Social Psychology* 92, no. 2 (2007): 325–36; and Gailliot and Baumeister, "The Physiology of Willpower," 303–27.

30. Gailliot and Baumeister, "The Physiology of Willpower," 303–27.

31. H. Andrea et al., "The Relation Between Pathological Worrying and Fatigue in a Working Population," *Journal of Psychosomatic Research* 57,

no. 4 (2004): 399–407, http://www.jpsychores.com/article/S0022 -3999(04)00048-0/abstract.

32. Sidney J. Blatt et al., "Dependency and Self-Criticism: Psychological Dimensions of Depression," *Journal of Consulting and Clinical Psychology* 50, no. 1 (1982): 113–24, http://psycnet.apa.org/journals/ccp/50/1/113/.

33. Veronika Job et al., "Ego Depletion—Is It All in Your Head? Implicit Theories About Willpower Affect Self-Regulation," *Psychological Science* 21, no. 11 (2010): 1686–93, DOI: 10.1177/0956797610384745.

34. J. J. Clarkson et al., "The Impact of Illusory Fatigue on Executive Control: Do Perceptions of Depletion Impair Working Memory Capacity?" *Social Psychological and Personality Science* 2, no. 3 (2010): 231–238, DOI: 10.1177/1948550610386628.

35. Chantal A. Arpin-Cribbie and Robert A. Cribbie, "Psychological Correlates of Fatigue: Examining Depression, Perfectionism, and Automatic Negative Thoughts," *Personality and Individual Differences* 43, no. 6 (2007): 1310–20, DOI: 10.1016/j.paid.2007.03.020.

36. Lorraine Maher-Edwards et al., "Metacognitions and Negative Emotions as Predictors of Symptom Severity in Chronic Fatigue Syndrome," *Journal of Psychosomatic Research* 70, no. 4 (2011): 311–17, http://www.sciencedirect.com/science/article/pii/S002239991000379X.

37. Andrew P. Hill and Thomas Curran, "Multidimensional Perfectionism and Burnout: A Meta-Analysis," *Personality and Social Psychology Review,* http://psr.sagepub.com/content/early/2015/07/25/1088868315596286.abstract.

38. Hill and Curran, "Multidimensional Perfectionism and Burnout."

39. Thomas S. Greenspon, "Is There an Antidote to Perfectionism?" *Psychology in the Schools* 51, no. 9 (2014): 986–98, DOI: 10.1002/pits.21797.

40. Kathleen Y. Kawamura et al., "Perfectionism, Anxiety, and Depression: Are the Relationships Independent?" *Cognitive Therapy and Research* 25, no. 25 (2001): 291–301, DOI: 10.1023/A:1010736529013.

41. Gordon L. Flett and Paul L. Hewitt, "The Perils of Perfectionism in Sports and Exercise," *Current Directions in Psychological Science* 14, no. 1 (2005): 14–18, DOI: 10.1111/j.0963-7214.2005.00326.x.

42. Barry Schwartz et al., "Maximizing Versus Satisficing: Happiness Is a Matter of Choice," *Journal of Personality and Social Psychology* 83, no. 5 (2002): 1178–97, DOI: 10.1037//0022-3514.83.5.1178.

43. Jeanne L. Tsai et al., "Influence and Adjustment Goals: Sources of Cultural Differences in Ideal Affect," *Journal of Personality and Social Psychology* 92, no. 6 (2007): 1100–17, DOI: 10.1037/0022-3514.92.6.1102.

44. W. Libby et al., "Pupillary and Cardiac Activity During Visual Attention," *Psychophysiology* 10 (1973): 270 –94; H. T. Schupp et al., "Probe P3 and Blinks: Two Measures of Affective Startle Modulation," *Psychophysiology* (1997): 34, 1– 6; Philip A. Gable, "Anger Perceptually and Conceptually Narrows Cognitive Scope," *Journal of Personality and Social Psychology* (forthcoming); Eddie Harmon-Jones et al., "Does Negative Affect Always Broaden the Mind? Considering the Influence of Motivational Intensity on Cognitive Scope," *Current Directions in Psychological Science* 22, no. 4 (2013): 301–7, DOI: 10.1177/0963721413481353; and Yaniv Hanoch and Oliver Vitouch, "When Less Is More: Information, Emotional Arousal and the Ecological Reframing of the Yerkes-Dodson Law," *Theory & Psychology* 14, no. 4 (2004): 427–52, DOI: 10.1177/0959354304044910.

45. N. A. S. Farb et al., "Attentional Modulation of Primary Interoceptive and Exteroceptive Cortices," *Cerebral Cortex* 23, no. 1: 114–26. DOI: 10.1093/cercor/bhr385.

46. Interview with Sarah Severn, August 6, 2015

47. M. Friese et al., "Mindfulness Meditation Counteracts Self-Control Depletion," *Consciousness and Cognition* 21, no. 2 (2012): 1016–22.

48. Stefan G. Hofman et al., "The Effect of Mindfulness-Based Therapy on Anxiety and Depression: A Meta-Analytic Review," *Journal of Consulting and Clinical Psychology* 78, no. 2 (2010): 169–83, http://psycnet .apa.org/?&fa=main.doiLanding&doi=10.1037/a0018555; Antoine Lutz et al., "Regulation of the Neural Circuitry of Emotion by Compas-

sion Meditation: Effects of Meditative Expertise," *PLoS ONE* 3, no. 3 (2008): 1897, DOI: 10.1371/journal.pone.0001897; and Rimma Teper et al., "Inside the Mindful Mind: How Mindfulness Enhances Emotion Regulation Through Improvements in Executive Control," *Current Directions in Psychological Science* 22, no. 6 (2013): 449–54, DOI: 10.1177/0963721413495869.

49. E. Harmon-Jones and C. K. Peterson, "Supine Body Position Reduces Neural Response to Anger Evocation: Short Report," *Psychological Science* 20, no. 10 (2009): 1209–10, DOI: 10.1111/j.1467-9280.2009 .02416.x.

50. Eileen Luders et al., "The Underlying Anatomical Correlates of Long-Term Meditation: Larger Hippocampal and Frontal Volumes of Gray Matter," *Neuroimage* 45 (2009): 672–78.

51. D. M. Tice et al., "Restoring the Self: Positive Affect Helps Improve Self-Regulation Following Ego Depletion," *Journal of Experimental Social Psychology* 43, no. 3 (2007): 379–84, DOI: 10.1016/j.jesp.2006 .05.007.

52. M. Friese and M. Wänke, "Personal Prayer Buffers Self-Control Depletion," *Journal of Experimental Social Psychology* 51 (2014): 56–59.

53. A. Grant, "Employees Without a Cause: The Motivational Effects of Prosocial Impact in Public Service," *International Public Management Journal,* vol. 11 (2008), 48–66, DOI: 10.1080/10967490801887905.

54. Akihito Shimazu et al., "Do Workaholism and Work Engagement Predict Employee Well-Being and Performance in Opposite Directions?," *Industrial Health* 50 (2012): 316–21, https://www.jstage.jst .go.jp/article/indhealth/50/4/50_MS1355/_pdf.

55. David DeSteno et al., "Gratitude: A Tool for Reducing Economic Impatience," *Psychological Science* 25, no. 6 (2014): 1262–67, DOI: 10.1177/0956797614529979.

56. S. Sonnentag et al., "Did You Have a Nice Evening? A Day-Level Study on Recovery Experiences, Sleep, and Affect," *Journal of Applied Psychology* 93 (2008): 674–84.

57. Interview with Sherron Lumley, April 15, 2015.

58. S. Sonnentag et al., "Job Stressors, Emotional Exhaustion, and Need for Recovery: A Multi-source Study on the Benefits of Psychological Detachment," *Journal of Vocational Behavior* 76 (2010): 355–65.

59. N. Feuerhahn et al., "Exercise After Work, Psychological Mediators, and Affect: A Day-Level Study," *European Journal of Work and Organizational Psychology* 23 (2014): 62–79.

60. S. Kaplan and M. G. Berman, "Directed Attention as a Common Resource for Executive Functioning and Self-Regulation," *Perspectives on Psychological Science* 5 (2010): 43–57.

61. V. Hahn et al., "The Role of Partners for Employees' Recovery During the Weekend," *Journal of Vocational Behavior* 80 (2012): 288–98.

CHAPTER 4: GET MORE DONE BY DOING MORE OF NOTHING

1. Interview with Myron Scholes, February 8, 2014.

2. David Z. Hambrick et al., "Deliberate Practice: Is That All It Takes to Become an Expert?," *Intelligence* 45 (2014): 34–45, DOI:10.1016/j.intell.2013.04.001.

3. "84 Percent of Executives Have Canceled a Vacation Due to 'Demands at Work' According to Korn Ferry Survey," Korn Ferry, June 13, 2014, http://www.kornferry.com/press/15179/.

4. Brandon Rottinghaus and Justin Vaughn, "New Ranking of U.S. Presidents Puts Lincoln at No. 1, Obama at 18; Kennedy Judged Most Overrated," *Washington Post,* February 16, 2015, http://www.washingtonpost.com/blogs/monkey-cage/wp/2015/02/16/new-ranking-of-u-s-presidents-puts-lincoln-1-obama-18-kennedy-judged-most-over-rated/.

5. "1000+ Reasons to Like Ike," *Golf Digest*, April 2008, http://www.golfdigest.com/golf-tours-news/2008-04/ike.

6. "IBM 2010 Global CEO Study: Creativity Selected as Most Crucial Factor for Future Success," press release, IBM, May 18, 2010, https://www-03.ibm.com/press/us/en/pressrelease/31670.wss.

7. W. Bernard Carlson, "Inventor of Dreams," *Scientific American* 78 (March 2015), http://www.teslauniverse.com/nikola-tesla-article-inventor-of-dreams.

8. Arthur I. Miller, "A Genius Finds Inspiration in the Music of Another," *New York Times*, January 31, 2006, http://www.nytimes.com/2006/01/31/science/31essa.html.

9. Alice Calaprice, ed., *The Expanded Quotable Einstein* (Princeton, NJ: Princeton University Press, 2000), 22, 287, and 10.

10. Cal Fussman, "Woody Allen: What I've Learned," *Esquire,* August 8, 2013, http://www.esquire.com/entertainment/interviews/a24203/woody-allen-0913/.

11. Elizabeth Gilbert, "Your Elusive Creative Genius," TED Talks, February 2009, https://www.ted.com/talks/elizabeth_gilbert_on_genius/transcript?language=en.

12. Interview with Scott Barry Kaufman, February 5, 2014.

13. B. Baird et al., "Inspired by Distraction: Mind Wandering Facilitates Creative Incubation," *Psychological Science* 23 (2012): 1117–22, DOI: 10.1177/0956797612446024.

14. Mareike B. Wieth and Rose T. Zacks, "Time of Day Effects on Problem Solving: When the Non-Optimal Is Optimal," *Thinking & Reasoning* 17 (2011): 387–401, DOI: 10.1080/13546783.2011.625663.

15. Salvador Dalí, *50 Secrets of Magic Craftsmanship* (New York: Dial Press, 1948), 36.

16. Interview with Scott Barry Kaufman, February 5, 2014.

17. Cindy Perman, "Inventions by Kids," CNBC, September 30, 2011, http://www.cnbc.com/id/42497934.

18. "Famous Pablo Picasso Quotes," Pablo Picasso: Paintings, Quotes, and Biography, http://www.pablopicasso.org/quotes.jsp.

19. George Land, "The Failure of Success," YouTube, December 2011, https://www.youtube.com/watch?v=ZfKMq-rYtnc; based on George Land and Beth Jarman, *Breaking Point and Beyond* (San Francisco: HarperBusiness, 1993).

20. Kyung Hee Kim, "The Creativity Crisis: The Decrease in Creative Thinking Scores on the Torrance Tests of Creative Thinking," *Creativity Research Journal* 23 (2011): 285–95, DOI: 10.1080/10400419.2011.627805.

21. Kyung Hee Kim, "Can Only Intelligent People Be Creative? A Meta-analysis," *Journal of Secondary Gifted Education* 16 (2005): 57–66, http://files.eric.ed.gov/fulltext/EJ698316.pdf.

22. Timothy D. Wilson et al., "Just Think: The Challenges of the Disengaged Mind," *Science* 4 (2014): 75–77, DOI: 10.1126/science.1250830.

23. Interview with Scott Barry Kaufman.

24. Marily Oppezzo and Daniel L. Schwartz, "Give Your Ideas Some Legs: The Positive Effect of Walking on Creative Thinking," *Journal of Experimental Psychology* 40, no. 4 (2014): 1142–52.

25. Kimberly D. Elsbach and Andrew B Hargadon, "Enhancing Creativity Through 'Mindless' Work: A Framework of Workday Design," *Organization Science* 17, no 4 (2006): 470–83.

26. Interview with Adam Grant, March 6, 2014.

27. Interview with Adam Grant, March 6, 2014.

28. Interview with Myron Scholes, February 8, 2014.

29. Karim R. Lakhani et al., "The Value of Openness in Scientific Problem Solving," HBS Working Paper 07-050, 2007, http://www.hbs.edu/faculty/Publication%20Files/07-050.pdf.

30. Cornelia Dean "If You Have a Problem, Ask Everyone," *New York Times,* July 22, 2008, http://www.nytimes.com/2008/07/22/science/22inno.html?_r=0.

31. Interview with Pico Iyer, January 12, 2014.

32. L. Bernardi et al., "Cardiovascular, Cerebrovascular and Respiratory Changes Induced by Different Types of Music in Musicians and Non-musicians: The Importance of Silence," *Heart* 92 (2006): 445–52, DOI: 10.1136/hrt.2005.064600.

33. I. Kirste et al., "Is Silence Golden? Effects of Auditory Stimuli and Their Absence on Adult Hippocampal Neurogenesis," *Brain Structure and Function* 220 (2015): 1221–28, DOI: 10.1007/s00429-013-0679-3.

34. "Recreation," Online Etymology Dictionary, http://www.etymonline
.com/index.php?term=recreation.

35. Darya L. Zabelina and Michael D. Robinson, "Child's Play: Facilitat-
ing the Originality of Creative Output by a Priming Manipulation,"
Psychology of Aesthetics, Creativity, and the Arts 4 (2010): 57–65, http://
psycnet.apa.org/index.cfm?fa=buy.optionToBuy&id=2010-03735-008.

36. Josh Dunlop, "Top 20 Most Awesome Company Offices," Income,
http://www.incomediary.com/top-20-most-awesome-company-offices.

37. B. L. Fredrickson and C. Branigan, "Positive Emotions Broaden the
Scope of Attention and Thought-Action Repertoires," *Cognition and
Emotion* 19 (2011): 313–32, DOI: 10.1080/02699930441000238.

38. E-mail exchange with Lolly Daskal, April 18, 2015.

39. Interview with Adam Grant, March 6, 2014.

CHAPTER 5: ENJOY A SUCCESSFUL RELATIONSHIP . . . WITH YOURSELF

1. Carol S. Dweck, *Self-Theories: Their Role in Motivation, Personality,
and Development* (New York: Psychology Press, 2000), 44–51; and
Carol S. Dweck, "Motivational Processes Affecting Learning,"
American Psychologist 41 (no. 10) (1986): 1040–48, DOI: 10.1037
/0003-066X.41.10.1040.

2. S. J. Blatt, "Representational Structures in Psychopathology," in *Roch-
ester Symposium on Developmental Psychopathology: Emotion, Cognition, and
Representation,* vol. 6, D. Cicchetti and S. Toth, ed. (Rochester, NY:
University of Rochester Press, 1995), 1–34.

3. Carl Marziali, "Brain Has Competing Risk and Reward," *USC News,*
October 9, 2008, http://news.usc.edu/29531/Brain-Has-Competing-
Risk-and-Reward/.

4. "Athletes' Fear of Failure Likely to Lead to 'Choke,' Study Shows,"
Coventry University, August 5, 2014, http://www.coventry.ac.uk
/primary-news/athletes-fear-of-failure-likely-to-lead-to-choke-
study-shows/.

5. Kristina Neff and Emma Seppälä, "Compassion, Well-Being and the Hypoegoic Self," in *Handbook of Hypo-egoic Phenomena,* ed. K. W. Brown and M. Leary (in press).

6. A. Michou et al., "Enriching the Hierarchical Model of Achievement Motivation: Autonomous and Controlling Reasons Underlying Achievement Goals," *British Journal of Educational Psychology* 84, no. 4 (2014): 650–66, DOI: 10.1111/bjep.12055.

7. Matthew S. Wood et al., "Take the Money or Run? Investors' Ethical Reputation and Entrepreneurs' Willingness to Partner," *Journal of Business Venturing* 29, no. 6 (2014): 723–40, http://dx.doi.org/10.1016/j .jbusvent.2013.08.004.

8. Roy F. Baumeister et al., "Bad Is Stronger Than Good," *Review of General Psychology* 5, no. 4 (2001): 323–70, DOI: 10.1037//1089-2680.5.4.323; and S. Gable and J. Haidt, "What (And Why) Is Positive Psychology," *Review of General Psychology* 9 (2005): 103–10, DOI: 10.1037/1089-2680.9.2.103.

9. Shelly L. Gable and Jonathan Haidt, "What (and Why) Is Positive Psychology?" *Review of General Psychology* 9, no. 2 (2005): 103–10, http://dx.doi.org/10.1037/1089-2680.9.2.103.

10. "Albert Einstein," in "Celebs Who Went from Failures to Success Stories," *CBS Money Watch,* http://www.cbsnews.com/pictures/celebs-who-went-from-failures-to-success-stories/3/; and Michael Michalko, "Famous Failures," *Creativity Post,* May 11, 2012, http://www.creativity post.com/psychology/famous_failures.

11. Carol S. Dweck and Ellen L. Leggett, "A Social-Cognitive Approach to Motivation and Personality," *Psychological Review* 85, no. 2 (1988): 256–73, http://dx.doi.org/10.1037/0033-295X.95.2.256.

12. Adi Ignatius, "Builders and Titans: Jack Ma," *Time,* April 30, 2009, http://content.time.com/time/specials/packages/article/0,28804 ,1894410_1893837_1894188,00.html.

13. William Mellor et al., "Ma Says Alibaba Shareholders Should Feel Love, Not No. 3," *Bloomberg Business,* November 9, 2014, http://www

.bloomberg.com/news/articles/2014-11-09/ma-says-alibaba-shareholders-should-feel-love-not-no-3.

14. Madeline Stone and Jillian D'Onfro, "The Inspiring Life Story of Alibaba Founder Jack Ma, Now the Richest Man in China," *Business Insider*, October 2, 2014, http://www.businessinsider.com/the-inspiring-life-story-of-alibaba-founder-jack-ma-2014-10.

15. Jeraldine Phneah, "8 Lessons to Learn from Jack Ma, Wealthiest Man in China," Jeraldine Phneah website, September 22, 2014, http://www.jeraldinephneah.me/2014/09/8-lessons-to-learn-from-jack-ma.html.

16. K. D. Neff, "Self-Compassion: An Alternative Conceptualization of a Healthy Attitude Toward Oneself," *Self and Identity* 2 (2010): 85–101.

17. K. D. Neff et al., "Self-Compassion and Its Link to Adaptive Psychological Functioning," *Journal of Research in Personality* 41 (2007): 139–54.

18. M. R. Leary, E. B. Tate, C. E. Adams, A. B. Allen, & J. Hancock, "Self-Compassion and Reactions to Unpleasant Self-Relevant Events: The Implications of Treating Oneself Kindly," *Journal of Personality and Social Psychology* 92 (2007): 887–904.

19. L. K. Barnard and J. F. Curry, "Self-Compassion: Conceptualizations, Correlates, and Interventions," *Review of General Psychology* 15 (2011): 289–303.

20. A. MacBeth and A. Gumley, "Exploring Compassion: A Meta-analysis of the Association Between Self-Compassion and Psychopathology," *Clinical Psychology Review* 32 (2012): 545–52.

21. L. Hollis-Walker and K. Colosimo, "Mindfulness, Self-Compassion, and Happiness in Non-meditators: A Theoretical and Empirical Examination," *Personality and Individual Differences* 50 (2011): 222–27; and Neff et al., "Self-Compassion and Its Link to Adaptive Psychological Functioning," 139–54.

22. J. G. Breines et al., "Self-Compassion as a Predictor of Interleukin-6 Response to Acute Psychosocial Stress," *Brain, Behavior, and Immunity* 37 (2014): 109–14, DOI: 10.1016/j.bbi.2013.11.006.

23. H. Rockliff et al., "A Pilot Exploration of Heart Rate Variability and Salivary Cortisol Responses to Compassion-Focused Imagery," *Clinical Neuropsychiatry* 5 (2008): 132–39.

24. S. W. Porges, "The Polyvagal Perspective," *Biological Psychology* 74 (2007): 116–43.

25. K. D. Neff et al., "Self-Compassion, Achievement Goals, and Coping with Academic Failure," *Self and Identity* 4 (2005): 263–87; and Neff et al., "Self-Compassion and Its Link to Adaptive Psychological Functioning," 139–54.

26. K. D. Neff and S. N. Beretvas, "The Role of Self-Compassion in Romantic Relationships," *Self and Identity* 12, no. 1 (2013): 78–98; and J. Crocker and A. Canevello, "Creating and Undermining Social Support in Communal Relationships: The Roles of Compassionate and Self-Image Goals," *Journal of Personality and Social Psychology* 95 (2008): 555–75.

27. M. E. Neely et al., "Self-Kindness When Facing Stress: The Role of Self-Compassion, Goal Regulation, and Support in College Students' Well-Being," *Motivation and Emotion* 33 (2009): 88–97.

28. C. E. Adams and M. R. Leary, "Promoting Self-Compassionate Attitudes Toward Eating Among Restrictive and Guilty Eaters," *Journal of Social and Clinical Psychology* 26 (2007): 1120–44; A. C. Kelly et al., "Who Benefits from Training in Self-Compassionate Self-Regulation? A Study of Smoking Reduction," *Journal of Social and Clinical Psychology* 29 (2009): 727–55; and C. Magnus et al., "The Role of Self-Compassion in Women's Self-Determined Motives to Exercise and Exercise-Related Outcomes," *Self and Identity* 9 (2010): 363–82.

29. M. R. Leary et al., "Self-Compassion and Reactions to Unpleasant Self-Relevant Events: The Implications of Treating Oneself Kindly," *Journal of Personality and Social Psychology* 92 (2007): 887–904.

30. P. Gilbert and C. Irons, "Focused Therapies and Compassionate Mind Training for Shame and Self-Attacking," in *Compassion: Conceptualisations, Research and Use in Psychotherapy,* ed. P. Gilbert (London: Routledge, 2005): 263–325.

31. "Tim Ryan," *Wall Street Journal,* http://projects.wsj.com/campaign2012/candidates/view/tim-ryan--OH-H.

32. Robert A. Emmons and Michael E. McCullough, "Counting Blessings Versus Burdens: An Experimental Investigation of Gratitude and Subjective Well-Being in Daily Life," *Journal of Personality and Social Psychology* 84, no. 2 (2003): 377–89, http://dx.doi.org/10.1037/0022-3514.84.2.377; Philip C. Watkins et al., "Gratitude and Happiness: Development of a Measure of Gratitude, and Relationships with Subjective Well-Being," *Social Behavior and Personality: An International Journal* 31, no. 5 (2003): 431–51, http://dx.doi.org/10.2224/sbp.2003.31.5.431; and Alex M. Wood et al., "Gratitude and Well-Being: A Review and Theoretical Integration," *Clinical Psychology Review* 30, no. 7 (2010): 890–905, DOI: 10.1016/j.cpr.2010.03.005.

33. Kennon M. Sheldon and Sonja Lyubomirsky, "How to Increase and Sustain Positive Emotion: The Effects of Expressing Gratitude and Visualizing Best Possible Selves," *Journal of Positive Psychology* 1, no. 2 (2006): 73–82, DOI: 10.1080/17439760500510676.

34. Alex M. Wood et al., "The Role of Gratitude in the Development of Social Support, Stress, and Depression: Two Longitudinal Studies," *Journal of Research in Personality* 42, no. 4 (2008): 854–71, DOI: 10.1016/j.jrp.2007.11.003.

35. Alex M. Wood et al., "The Role of Gratitude in the Development of Social Support, Stress, and Depression: Two Longitudinal Studies," *Journal of Research in Personality* 42, no. 4 (2008): 854–71, DOI: 10.1016/j.jrp.2007.11.003.

36. Emily L. Polak and Michael E. McCullough, "Is Gratitude an Alternative to Materialism?" *Journal of Happiness Studies* 7, no. 3 (2006): 343–60.

37. Tori DeAngelis, "Consumerism and Its Discontents," *American Psychological Association* 35, no. 6 (2004): 52.

38. Alex M. Wood et al., "Gratitude Influences Sleep Through the Mechanism of Pre-sleep Cognitions," *Journal of Psychosomatic Research* 66, no. 1 (2009): 43–48, DOI: 10.1016/j.jpsychores.2008.09.002.

39. Alex M. Wood et al., "Gratitude Uniquely Predicts Satisfaction with Life: Incremental Validity Above the Domains and Facets of the Five Factor Model," *Personality and Individual Differences* 45, no. 1 (2008): 49–54, DOI: 10.1016/j.paid.2008.02.019.

40. Sara B. Algoe et al., "Beyond Reciprocity: Gratitude and Relationships in Everyday Life," *Emotion* 8, no. 3 (2008): 425–29, http://dx.doi .org/10.1037/1528-3542.8.3.425; Sara B. Algoe and Jonathan Haidt, "Witnessing Excellence in Action: The 'Other-Praising' Emotions of Elevation, Gratitude, and Admiration," *Journal of Positive Psychology* 4, no. 2 (2009): 105–27, DOI: 10.1080/17439760802650519; Nathaniel M. Lambert et al., "Benefits of Expressing Gratitude: Expressing Gratitude to a Partner Changes One's View of the Relationship," *Psychological Science* 21, no. 4 (2010): 574–80, DOI: 10.1177/0956797610364003; and Sara B. Algoe, "Find, Remind, and Bind: The Functions of Gratitude in Everyday Relationships," *Social and Personality Psychology Compass* 6, no. 6 (2012): 455–59, DOI: 10.1111/j.1751-9004.2012.00439.

41. Michael E. McCullough et al., "Is Gratitude a Moral Affect?" *Psychological Bulletin* 127, no. 2 (2001): 249–66, http://dx.doi.org/10 .1037/0033-2909.127.2.249; Michael E. McCullough et al., "An Adaptation for Altruism: The Social Causes, Social Effects, and Social Evolution of Gratitude," *Psychological Science* 17, no. 4 (2008): 281–85, DOI: 10.1111/j.1467-8721.2008.00590; and Monica Y. Bartlett and David DeSteno, "Gratitude and Prosocial Behavior: Helping When It Costs You," *Psychological Science* 17, no. 4 (2006): 319–25, DOI: 10.1111/j.1467-9280.2006.01705.

42. Robert A. Emmons and Cheryl A. Crumpler, "Gratitude as a Human Strength: Appraising the Evidence," *Journal of Social and Clinical Psychology* 19, no. 1 (2000): 56–69, DOI: 10.1521/jscp.2000.19.1.56.

43. David DeSteno et al., "Gratitude: A Tool for Reducing Economic Impatience," *Psychological Science* 25 (2014): 1262–67, DOI: 10.1177 /0956797614529979.

44. McCullough et al., "Is Gratitude a Moral Affect?," 249–66; and McCullough et al., "Adaptation for Altruism," 281–85.

45. Adam A. Grant and Francesca Gino, "A Little Thanks Goes a Long Way: Explaining Why Gratitude Expressions Motivate Prosocial Behavior," *Journal of Personality and Social Psychology* 98, no. 6 (2010): 946–55, DOI: 10.1037/a0017935.

46. Emiliana R. Simon-Thomas and Jeremy Adam Smith, "How Grateful Are Americans?" *Greater Good: The Science of a Meaningful Life,* January 10, 2013, http://greatergood.berkeley.edu/article/item/how_grateful _are_americans.

47. Amit Bhattacharjee and Cassie Mogilner, "Happiness from Ordinary and Extraordinary Experiences," *Journal of Consumer Research* 41 (2014): 1–17.

48. Natali Moyal et al., "Cognitive Strategies to Regulate Emotions— Current Evidence and Future Directions," *Frontiers in Psychology* 4 (2014): 1019, DOI: 10.3389/fpsyg.2013.01019.

49. Alex M. Wood et al., "Gratitude and Well-Being: A Review and Theoretical Integration," *Clinical Psychology Review* 30, no. 7 (2010): 890–905, DOI: 10.1016/j.cpr.2010.03.005.

CHAPTER 6: UNDERSTAND THE KINDNESS EDGE

1. Henry David Thoreau, *The Writings of Henry David Thoreau,* Vol. 2 (Houghton Mifflin, 1906), 241.

2. Name changed for anonymity.

3. "People and Events: Herbert Spencer," *American Experience,* http:// www.pbs.org/wgbh/amex/carnegie/peopleevents/pande03.html.

4. Jennifer L. Goetz et al., "Compassion: An Evolutionary Analysis and Empirical Review," *Psychological Bulletin* 136, no. 3 (2010): 351–74, DOI: 10.1037/a0018807.

5. Sydney Ember, "Remembering Ace Greenberg, Through Good Times and Bad," *New York Times,* July 25, 2014, http://dealbook.nytimes .com/2014/07/25/remembering-ace-greenberg-through-good-times- and-bad/?ref=topics.

6. Jody Shenn and Bradley Keoun, "Bear Stearns Rivals Reject Fund Bailout in LTCM Redux (Update 3)," Bloomberg, June 25, 2007, http://www.bloomberg.com/apps/news?pid=newsarchive&sid=aYDTe HYnV3ms.

7. Andrew Ross Sorkin, "JP Morgan Raises Bid for Bear Stearns to $10 a share," *New York Times*, March 17, 2008, http://www.nytimes .com/2008/03/24/business/24deal-web.html?pagewanted=all.

8. J. M. Twenge et al., "Egos Inflating over Time: A Cross-Temporal Meta-analysis of the Narcissistic Personality Inventory," *Journal of Personality* 76 (2008): 875–902.

9. Interview with Jean Twenge, June 2, 2015.

10. Timothy A. Judge et al., "Loving Yourself Abundantly: Relationship of the Narcissistic Personality to Self- and Other Perceptions of Work-place Deviance, Leadership, and Task and Contextual Performance," *Journal of Applied Psychology* 9, no. 4 (2006): 762–76, DOI: 10.1037 /0021-9010.91.4.762.

11. R. F. Baumeister et al., "Relation of Threatened Egotism to Violence and Aggression: The Dark Side of High Self-Esteem," *Psychological Review* 103 (1996): 5–33; and J. M. Twenge and W. K. Campbell, "'Isn't It Fun to Get the Respect That We're Going to Deserve?': Narcissism, Social Rejection and Aggression," *Personality and Social Psychology Bulletin* 29 (2003): 261–72.

12. Lisa M. Penney and Paul E. Spector, "Narcissism and Counterproduc-tive Work Behavior: Do Bigger Egos Mean Bigger Problems?" *International Journal of Selection and Assessment* 10, nos. 1–2 (2002): 126–34, DOI: 10.1111/1468-2389.00199.

13. C. Salmivalli et al., "Self-Evaluated Self-Esteem, Peer-Evaluated Self-Esteem, and Defensive Egotism as Predictors of Adolescents' Participa-tion in Bullying Situations," *Personality and Social Psychology Bulletin* 25 (1999): 1268–78; S. Fein and S. J. Spencer, "Prejudice as Self-Image Maintenance: Affirming the Self Through Derogating Others," *Journal of Personality and Social Psychology* 73 (1997): 31–44; and J. Crocker et al., "Downward Comparison, Prejudice, and Evaluations of Others: Effects

of Self-Esteem and Threat," *Journal of Personality and Social Psychology* 52 (1987): 907–16.

14. R. F. Baumeister and M. R. Leary, "The Need to Belong: Desire for Interpersonal Attachments as a Fundamental Human Motivation," *Psychological Bulletin* 117, no. 3 (1995): 497–529.

15. Interview with Adam Grant, March 6, 2014.

16. Kristi M. Lewis, "When Leaders Display Emotion: How Followers Respond to Negative Emotional Expression of Male and Female Leaders," *Journal of Organizational Behavior* 21, no. 2 (2000): 221–34, DOI: 10.1002/(SICI)1099-1379(200003)21:2<221::AID-JOB36>3.0.CO;2-0.

17. Sunday Azagba and Mesbah F. Sharaf, "Psychosocial Working Conditions and the Utilization of Health Care Services," *BMC Public Health* 11 (2011): 642, DOI: 10.1186/1471-2458-11-642.

18. R. S. Bridger et al., "Occupational Stress and Employee Turnover," *Ergonomics* 56, no. 11 (2013): 1629–39, DOI: 10.1080/00140139 .2013.836251.

19. Kristin Neff, "Self-Compassion: An Alternative Conceptualization of a Healthy Attitude Toward Oneself," *Self and Identity* 2, no. 2 (2003): 85–101, DOI: 10.1080/15298860390129863.

20. V. Hoorens, "Self-Enhancement and Superiority Biases in Social Comparison," *European Review of Social Psychology* 4 (1993): 113–39, DOI: 10.1080/14792779343000040.

21. S. H. Heine et al., "Is There a Universal Need for Positive Self-Regard?" *Psychological Review* 106 (1999): 766–94; and C. Sedikides, "Assessment, Enhancement, and Verification Determinants of the Self-Evaluation Process," *Journal of Personality and Social Psychology* 65 (1993): 317–38.

22. J. Crocker et al., "Contingencies of Self-Worth in College Students: Theory and Measurement," *Journal of Personality and Social Psychology* 85 (2003): 894–908.

23. R. F. Baumeister et al., "Does High Self-Esteem Cause Better Performance, Interpersonal Success, Happiness, or Healthier Lifestyles?" *Psychological Science in the Public Interest* 4 (2003): 1–44.

24. L. Scherwitz and J. Canick, "Self Reference and Coronary Heart Disease Risk," in *Type A Behavior Pattern: Research, Theory, and Intervention*, ed. K. Houston and C. R. Snyder (New York: Wiley, 1988), 146–67; and L. Scherwitz et al., "Self-Involvement and the Risk Factor for Coronary Heart Disease," *Advances* 2 (1985): 6–18.

25. N. Mor and J. Winquist, "Self-Focused Attention and Negative Affect: A Meta-analysis," *Psychological Bulletin* 128, no. 4 (2002): 638–62.

26. J. F. Coutinho, "Default Mode Network Dissociation in Depressive and Anxiety States," *Brain Imaging Behavior* (2015), http://link.springer.com/article/10.1007/s11682-015-9375-7.

27. S. Tanaka et al., "The Relationship Among Self-Focused Attention, Depression, and Anxiety," *Shinrigaku Kenkyu* 78, no. 4 (2007): 365–71, http://www.ncbi.nlm.nih.gov/pubmed/18027582.

28. Coutinho, "Default Mode Network Dissociation in Depressive and Anxiety States."

29. J. S. House et al., "Social Relationships and Health," *Science* 241 (1988): 540–45.

30. J. T. Hawkley and J. T. Cacioppo, "Aging and Loneliness: Downhill Quickly?" *Current Directions in Psychological Science* 16 (2007): 187–91.

31. Louise C. Hawkley and John T. Cacioppo, "Loneliness Matters: A Theoretical and Empirical Review of Consequences and Mechanisms," *Annals of Behavioral Medicine* 40, no. 2 (2010): 218–27, DOI: 10.1007/s12160-010-9210-8.

32. Richard M. Lee et al., "Social Connectedness, Dysfunctional Interpersonal Behaviors, and Psychological Distress: Testing a Mediator Model," *Journal of Counseling Psychology* 48, no. 3 (2001): 310–18, http://psycnet.apa.org/index.cfm?fa=buy.optionToBuy&id=2001-07409-008.

33. Jennifer L. Goetz et al., "Compassion: An Evolutionary Analysis and Empirical Review," *Psychological Bulletin* 136, no. 3 (2010): 351–74, DOI: 10.1037/a0018807.

34. Inbal Ben-Ami Bartal et al., "Helping a Cagemate in Need: Empathy and Pro-social Behavior in Rats," *Science* 334, no. 6061 (2011): 1427–30, DOI: 10.1126/science.1210789.

35. Felix Warneken and Michael Tomasello, "Altruistic Helping in Human Infants and Young Chimpanzees," *Science* 311, no. 5765 (2006): 1301–3, DOI: 10.1126/science.1121448.

36. Interview with Brené Brown, January 23, 2012.

37. Ethan Kross et al., "Social Rejection Shares Somatosensory Representations with Physical Pain," *Proceedings of the National Academy of Sciences of the United States of America* 108, no. 15 (2011): 6270–75, DOI: 10.1073/pnas.1102693108.

38. G. M. Slavich et al., "Neural Sensitivity to Social Rejection Is Associated with Inflammatory Responses to Social Stress," *Proceedings of the National Academy of Sciences of the United States of America* 107, no. 33 (2010): 14817–22, DOI: 10.1073/pnas.1009164107.

39. "Volunteering in the United States, 2014," Bureau of Labor Statistics, February 25, 2015, http://www.bls.gov/news.release/volun.nr0.htm.

40. Paul K. Kraus et al., "Having Less, Giving More: The Influence of Social Class on Prosocial Behavior," *Journal of Personality and Social Psychology* 99, no. 5 (2010): 771–84, http://socrates.berkeley.edu/~keltner/publications/piff.2010.pdf.

41. J. Moll et al., "Human Fronto-Mesolimbic Networks Guide Decisions About Charitable Donation," *Proceedings of the National Academy of Sciences* 103, no. 42 (2006): 15623–28.

42. Elizabeth W. Dunn et al., "Spending Money on Others Promotes Happiness," *Science* 319, no. 5870 (2008): 1687–88, DOI: 10.1126/science.1150952.

43. L. B. Aknin et al., "Giving Leads to Happiness in Young Children," *PLoS ONE* 7, no. 6 (2012): e39211, DOI: 10.1371/journal.pone.0039211.

44. Robert H. Frank et al., "Does Studying Economics Inhibit Cooperation?" *Journal of Economic Perspectives* 7, no. 2 (1993): 159–71, DOI: 10.1257/jep.7.2.159.

45. Kim Cameron et al., "Effects of Positive Practices on Organizational Effectiveness," *Journal of Applied Behavioral Science* 47, no. 3 (2011): 266–308, DOI: 10.1177/0021886310395514.

46. Sigal Barsade and Donald E. Gibson, "Why Does Affect Matter in Organizations?" *Academy of Management Perspectives* 21 (2007): 36–59, http://www.donaldegibson.com/files/Why Does Affect Matter.pdf.

47. Sigal G. Barsade and Olivia A. O'Neill, "What's Love Got to Do with It? A Longitudinal Study of the Culture of Companionate Love and Employee and Client Outcomes in the Long-Term Care Setting," *Administrative Science Quarterly* 20, no. 20 (2014): 1–48, DOI: 10.1177/0001839214538636.

48. Charlie L. Hardy and Mark Van Vugt, "Nice Guys Finish First: The Competitive Altruism Hypothesis," *Personality and Social Psychology Bulletin* 32, no. 10 (2006): 1402–13, DOI: 10.1177/014616720629 1006.

49. Amy J. C. Cuddy et al., "Connect, Then Lead," *Harvard Business Review* (July–August 2013), https://hbr.org/2013/07/connect-then-lead/ar/1.

50. Luke Norman et al., "Attachment-Security Priming Attenuates Amygdala Activation to Social and Linguistic Threat," *Social Cognitive and Affective Neuroscience* 10, no. 6 (2015): 832–39, DOI: 10.1093/scan/nsu127.

51. Fiona Lee et al., "The Mixed Effects of Inconsistency on Experimentation in Organizations," *Organization Science* 15, no. 3 (2004): 310–26, http://pubsonline.informs.org/doi/abs/10.1287/orsc.1040.0076?journal Code=orsc.

52. Brené Brown, "The Power of Vulnerability," TED Talks, June 2010, https://www.ted.com/talks/brene_brown_on_vulnerability?language =en.

53. Transformational Leadership for Excellence, http://tlexinstitute.com/.

54. Interview with Johann Berlin, November 15, 2014.

55. Michelangelo Vianello et al., "Elevation at Work: The Effects of Leaders' Moral Excellence," *Journal of Positive Psychology* 5, no. 5 (2010): 390–411, DOI: 10.1080/17439760.2010.516764.

56. Tianjiao Qiu et al., "The Effect of Interactional Fairness on the Performance of Cross-Functional Product Development Teams: A Multilevel Mediated Model," *Journal of Product Innovation Management* 26, no. 2 (2009): 173–87, DOI: 10.1111/j.1540-5885.2009.00344.x.

57. Wayne E. Baker and Nathaniel Bulkley, "Paying It Forward Versus Rewarding Reputation: Mechanisms of Generalized Reciprocity," Ross School of Business Paper no. 1236, *Organization Science* (2014), http://papers.ssrn.com/sol3/papers.cfm?abstract_id=2429752.

58. Interview with Archana Patchirajan, November 28, 2014.

59. "Britain's Workers Value Companionship and Recognition over a Big Salary, a Recent Report Revealed," AAT, https://www.aat.org.uk/about-aat/press-releases/britains-workers-value-companionship-recognition-over-big-salary.

60. J. Holt-Lunstad et al., "Social Relationships and Mortality Risk: A Meta-analytic Review," *PLoS Med.* 7, no. 7 (2010): 31000316, DOI: 10.1371/journal.pmed.1000316.

61. Sheldon Cohen and Thomas Ashby Wills, "Stress, Social Support, and the Buffering Hypothesis," *Psychological Bulletin* 98, no. 2 (1985): 310-357, http://lchc.ucsd.edu/MCA/Mail/xmcamail.2012_11.dir/pdf YukILvXsL0.pdf.

62. Sarah D. Pressman et al., "Loneliness, Social Network Size and Immune Response to Influenza Vaccination in College Freshmen," *Health Psychology* 24, no. 3 (2005): 297–306, DOI: 10.1037/0278-6133.24.3.297.

63. J. C. Hawkley et al., "Effects of Social Isolation on Glucocorticoid Regulation in Social Mammals," *Hormones & Behavior* 62 (2012): 314–23, DOI: 10.1016/j.yhbeh.2012.05.011.

64. Richard M. Lee et al., "Social Connectedness, Dysfunctional Interpersonal Behaviors, and Psychological Distress: Testing a Mediator Model," *Journal of Counseling Psychology* 48, no. 3 (2001): 310–18, http://psycnet.apa.org/index.cfm?fa=buy.optionToBuy&id=2001-07409-008.

65. Michael J. Poulin et al., "Giving to Others and the Association Between Stress and Mortality," *American Journal of Public Health* 103, no. 9 (2013): 1649–55, DOI: 10.2105/AJPH.2012.300876.

66. S. L. Brown et al., "Caregiving Behavior Is Associated with Decreased Mortality Risk," *Psychological Science* 20, no. 4 (2009): 488–94, DOI: 10.1111/j.1467-9280.2009.02323.x.

67. Paula M. Niedenthal, "Embodying Emotion," *Science* 316, no. 5827 (2007): 1002–5, DOI: 10.1126/science.1136930.

68. Philip L. Jackson et al., "How Do We Perceive the Pain of Others? A Window into the Neural Processes Involved in Empathy," *NeuroImage* 24, no. 3 (2005): 771–79, DOI: 10.1016/j.neuroimage.2004.09.006.

69. Simon Baron-Cohen et al., "The 'Reading the Mind in the Eyes' Test Revised Version: A Study with Normal Adults, and Adults with Asperger Syndrome or High-Functioning Autism," *Journal of Child Psychology and Psychiatry* 42, no. 2 (2001): 241–51, DOI: 10.1111/1469-7610.00715.

70. B. L. Fredrickson et al., "Open Hearts Build Lives: Positive Emotions, Induced Through Loving-Kindness Meditation, Build Consequential Personal Resources," *Journal of Personality and Social Psychology* 95, no. 5 (2008): 1045–62, DOI: 10.1037/a0013262; T. W. Pace et al., "Effect of Compassion Meditation on Neuroendocrine, Innate Immune and Behavioral Responses to Psychosocial Stress," *Psychoneuroendocrinology* 34 (2009): 87–98, DOI: 10.1016/j.psyneuen.2008.08.011; and T. W. Pace et al., "Engagement with Cognitively-Based Compassion Training Is Associated with Reduced Salivary C-Reactive Protein from Before to After Training in Foster Care Program Adolescents," *Psychoneuroendocrinology* 38 (2013): 294–99, DOI: 10.1016/j.psyneuen.2012.05.019.

71. J. S. Mascaro et al., "Compassion Meditation Enhances Empathic Accuracy and Related Neural Activity," *Social Cognitive and Affective Neuroscience* 8, no. 1 (2013): 48–55, DOI: 10.1093/scan/nss095.

72. C. A. Hutcherson et al., "The Neural Correlates of Social Connection," *Cognitive and Affective Behavioral Neuroscience* 15 (2015): 1–14, DOI: 10.3758/s13415-014-0304-9.

73. S. Leiberg et al., "Short-Term Compassion Training Increases Prosocial Behavior in a Newly Developed Prosocial Game," *PLoS ONE* 6 (2011), DOI: 10.1371/journal.pone.0017798.

74. Mascaro et al., "Compassion Meditation," 48–55; A. Lutz et al., "Regulation of the Neural Circuitry of Emotion by Compassion Meditation: Effects of Meditative Expertise," *PLoS ONE* 3 (2008): e1897, DOI: 10.1371/journal.pone.0001897; M. E. Kemeny et al., "Contemplative/Emotion Training Reduces Negative Emotional Behavior and Promotes Prosocial Responses," *Emotion* 12 (2012): 338–50, DOI: 10.1037/a0026118; Gaelle Desbordes et al., "Effects of Mindful-Attention and Compassion Meditation Training on Amygdala Response to Emotional Stimuli in an Ordinary, Non-meditative State," *Frontiers in Human Neuroscience* 6 (2012): 292, DOI: 10.3389/fnhum.2012.00292; and H. Jazaieri et al., "A Randomized Controlled Study of Compassion Cultivation Training: Effects on Mindfulness, Affect and Emotion Regulation," *Motivation and Emotion* 38 (2014): 23–35, DOI: 10.1007/s11031-013-9368-z.

75. C. A. Hutcherson et al., "Loving-Kindness Meditation Increases Social Connectedness," *Emotion* 5 (2008): 720–24, DOI: 10.1037/a0013237.

INDEX

addiction, 21, 51
  stress and, 51, 53–54
  work, 18–24
adrenaline, 50, 57, 58, 82
advertising, 50
aging, 147, 148, 160–61
alcohol, 51, 53, 77
  stress and, 53, 54
Allen, Woody, 99
alternate nostril breathing, 63
Angelou, Maya, 1
anger, 8, 9, 29, 56, 62, 71,
    145–46
anticipatory joy, 20–22, 23
antidepressants, 7
anxiety, 7, 10, 15–16, 23, 26, 29,
    44–45, 56, 71, 83, 86, 88, 122,
    126, 134, 160, 163
  breathing and, 56–63
  resilience and, 39–66
athletes, 59, 65–66
attention deficit hyperactivity
    disorder, 97

Baumeister, Roy, 74, 75, 76, 77,
    85, 88, 127
Bear Stearns, 141–42, 143 152–53

Beeman, Mark, 8
Beethoven, Ludwig van, 98–99
Berkman, Elliot, 70, 79, 90, 93
Berlin, Johann, 157
Bernardi, Luciano, 111
big picture, remembering the,
    91–92
blind spots, and self-focus, 144–45
blood sugar, 77
boredom, 71, 105
brain, 8, 20–21, 25, 47–48, 72,
    100, 112, 126, 151, 162
  creative thinking, 99–101
  excitement and, 72–73
  impact of thoughts reduced by
    calm, 85–87
  multitasking and, 25–26
  negativity bias, 127–28
  neural systems, 100, 129
  stress and, 44–45, 156
breathing, 35, 55–63
  alternate nostril, 63
  exercises, 35, 59–63, 89
  focus, 35
  resilience and, 55–63
  stress and, 55–63
Brilliant, Larry, 88

broadening horizons, diversifying
through, 109–10, 117–18
Brown, Brené, 149, 157
bullying, 146
burnout, 68–69, 83

Cadello, Armand, 48–49
caffeine, 51, 54, 82, 86
calm, 12, 60, 61, 67–94
  cultivation of, 87–90
  hidden benefits of, 67–94
  impact of thoughts reduced by,
    85–87
  as key to energy management,
    80–90
  self-control and, 84–85
Cameron, Kim, 154
catastrophizing, 78–79
Cayne, Jimmy, 143
cell phones, 21, 30, 36
charisma, 30–33
  being present increases your,
    30–33
charity, 151
"chase" mentality, 20–22
children, 46, 85, 102, 120, 142,
  149, 151
  creativity in, 102, 104
  resilience in, 46, 47
  self-beliefs of, 123–24
China, 86, 91, 124, 130
Christakis, Nicolas, 10, 158
cigarettes, 53, 147
college, 4, 15–18, 92, 114, 121–
  22, 130, 137, 139, 142

narcissism and, 144, 145
semester abroad, 109
success and, 15–18
Columbia University, 4
compassion, 11, 12, 133, 141–64
  for others, 141–64
  loyalty and engagement, 157–60
  physical health and, 160–61
  self-, 131–40
  self-focus vs., 143–48
  status and trustworthiness,
    155–57
  strengthening, 161–64
  success and, 148–61
  training, 163–64
  work and, 141–47, 152–61
competition, 5, 142
concentration, 96, 97, 119
Confucius, 91
control, 87
  self-, 70, 73–77, 84–85, 88
cortisol, 11, 59–60, 134
creativity, 8, 11, 29, 95–120, 134
  buried by education, 102–4
  fun and, 113–17, 119–20
  idleness and, 95–120
  lack of, 101 6
  making time for idleness,
    117–20
  no time for, 104–6
  power of, 98–99
  stillness and silence for, 110–13,
    118–19
  three paths to creative idleness,
    106–17

unfocusing through diversification, 107–10, 117–18
work and, 98–99, 116, 118
Csíkszentmihályi, Mihály, 27
"cuddle hormone," 134–35, 151
Cuddy, Amy, 156

Dalí, Salvador, 101
Darwin, Charles, 142, 143
Daskal, Lolly, 116
daydreaming, 29, 99–102, 105, 107
deadlines, 2, 128
delayed gratification, 19
depression, 9, 10, 26, 51, 83, 122, 125, 126, 134, 160, 163
Dhabhar, Firdaus, 43
discipline, 73–77
distractions, 74
divergent thinking, 102–3
diversification, unfocus through, 107–10, 117–18
Dobberke, Jake, 57–58, 61
dopamine, 20–21
drive, 39–41
drugs, 51
Dweck, Carol, 79, 123, 124, 129–30

economics, 95–96, 143, 152
education, creativity buried by, 102–4
effort, believe in, 129–31
Einstein, Albert, 99, 114, 129
Eisenhower, Dwight, 97–98

elation, 71, 72
elevation, 157–58
Elsbach, Kimberly, 108
e-mail, 2–3, 21, 29, 48–49, 82, 104
stress and, 48–49
embodied cognition, 89
empathy, 31, 149, 161–64
energy, 12, 67–94
big picture and, 91–92
burnout, 68–69, 83
calm as key to management of, 80–90
cost of intensity, 70–80
management, 67–94
preservation of, 81–84
restoring mental energy, 90–94
energy drinks, 51, 54, 82
engagement, and compassion, 157–60
enthusiasm, 32
excitement, 71–73, 82
exercise, 64–65, 76, 89, 113, 118, 120
breathing, 35, 59–63
slow-paced, 65
stress and, 59
extrinsic motivation, 92
eye contact, 31–32, 162–63

Facebook, 3, 15, 20, 21, 74, 105, 108, 115
facial expressions, 162–63
failure, 6, 121–24, 126, 129, 130, 133, 146

failure *(continued)*
  fear of, 125–29, 134
  self-focus and, 146–47
fame, 22
fatigue, 5, 70, 85
  beliefs about, 79–80
  as cost of intensity, 70–80
  self-control, 73–77
fear, 29, 44–45, 56, 71
  irrational, 79
Federal Reserve Bank, 143
fight-or-flight response, 45–46, 57,
    58, 60, 72, 134
flow, 27
focus, 5, 6, 84, 96, 97, 100, 108,
    109, 119
  self-, 143–48
food, 35, 53–54, 64, 75, 76
  diets, 75
  stress and, 53, 54
Forbes, 17
Ford, Bill, 88
forgiveness, 154
Fowler, James, 10, 158
France, 1–2
Fredrickson, Barbara, 8, 9, 10, 115
frustration, 20
fun, 113–17, 119–20
future, stop chasing the, 15–37

Gable, Shelley, 127
games, 120
Gates, Bill, 125
Gilbert, Daniel, 22, 28, 29, 33
Gilbert, Elizabeth, 99

Gilbert, Paul, 48, 134
givers and takers, 155–56
Gladwell, Malcolm, 96
golf, 97
Google, 15, 115
Gracie, Royce, 67
Grant, Adam, 91, 108, 109, 117,
    146, 155
Give and Take, 155–56
gratitude, 135–39
  daily list, 139
  practicing, 93
Great Britain, 81
Gross, James, 53

habituation, 128
Haidt, Jonathan, 127, 157–58
Hanh, Thich Nhat, 39
happiness, 2, 7–13, 99, 151
  in the present, 15–37
  success and, 4–13
Hargadon, Andrew, 108
heart disease, 147
heart rate, 134, 151
Heitmann, Mike, 67–68, 69
high-intensity emotions, 70,
    71 73, 81, 82
high-intensity negative thoughts,
    70, 77–80
hormones, 134, 151
  "cuddle," 134–35, 151
  stress, 11, 59–60, 134, 163
Horta-Osório, António, 39–42,
    44, 65
House, James S., 148

hugs, 65
hypnagogia, 101

idleness, 12, 95–120
  creativity and, 95–120
  fun and, 113–17, 119–20
  making time for, 117–20
  mind and, 99–120
  stillness and silence, 110–13,
    118–19
  unfocus through diversification,
    107–10, 117–18
immune system, 10, 11, 43, 148,
  160, 163
India, 158–59
individualism, 147
inflammation, 10, 11, 44, 134,
  148, 160, 163
Innocentive, 110
intellect, and happiness, 8
intensity, cost of, 70–80
internal awareness, 85–87
Internet, 2–3, 130
intrinsic motivation, 92
intuition, 99
investment banking, 141–42, 143,
  152–54
IQ, 103, 104
ironic processes, 77
Iyer, Pico, 111, 112, 113
  The Art of Stillness, 111

Japan, 124
joy, 99, 113–17
  anticipatory, 20–23

jujitsu, 67–68

Kaufman, Scott Barry, 100, 101,
  107–8, 109
Kekulé, Friedrich August, 98
Killingsworth, Matthew, 28, 29,
  33
Kim, Kyung-Hee, 103–4
kindness, 141–64

Lakhani, Karim, 110
Land, George, 103
  Grow or Die, 103
Lao Tzu, 121
laughter, 9, 10
Lee, Fiona, 156
Limaye, Tanuja, 83–84
linear thinking, 100, 102–4, 106
LinkedIn, 3, 21, 25
listening, 31, 162–63
Lloyds Banking Group, 39, 40–41,
  44, 65
Loehr (Jim) and Schwartz (Tony),
  The Power of Full Engagement, 67
love, 35
loyalty, and compassion, 157–60
Lumley, Sherron, 93

Ma, Jack, 130–31
Macy, R. H., 125
Mark, Gloria, 48–49
martial arts, 67–68
massage, 35
materialism, 136, 144
Max Planck Institute, 149

Mayo Clinic, 69
meditation, 34–35, 60, 87–90, 111, 112, 113, 118, 119
  calm cultivated with, 87–90
  exercises, 88–90
memory, 25–26, 44, 100, 101
mind, 47–49, 80
  beliefs about fatigue, 79–80
  breathing and, 55–63
  bringing your mind into the present, 33–37
  calm as key to energy management, 80–90
  control, 74
  excitement and, 72–73
  high-intensity thoughts, 77–80
  idleness and, 99–120
  as resilience saboteur, 47–49
  restoring mental energy, 90–94
  wandering, 28–29, 33, 34, 35, 99–120
mindfulness, 11, 34–35, 132–33
mindless tasks, diversifying with, 107–9
mistakes, 132, 133
money, 22, 23, 136, 141–42, 144, 151
morning mortality effect, 76
Mozart, Wolfgang Amadeus, 99
multitasking, 24–26
music, 98, 99, 111, 118

narcissism, 143–48
NASA, 103, 110
nature, 119

Neff, Kristin, 126, 132, 133, 138, 139
negativity bias, 127–28, 135, 138
nervous system, 11, 46, 78, 134
  breathing and, 55–65
  easing into your body, 64–65
  stress and, 46, 50–65
niche, focus on, 5
9/11 attacks, 44
nonlinear thinking, 95–120
nonprofit organizations, 16, 17, 69

optimism, 9, 53, 134
overachievement, 18–24
overdrive, stepping out of, 39–66
oxytocin, 134–35, 151

Paris, 1, 2
Patchirajan, Archie, 158–59
peacefulness, 71
perfectionism, 83
Perlow, Leslie, *Sleeping with Your Smartphone,* 21
Pertofsky, Carole, 17–18
Philippot, Pierre, 55–56
physical affection, 65
physical health, 9–10, 23, 27–28, 40, 64–65, 134
  compassion and, 160–61
  happiness, 9–10
  overachievement and, 23
  self-focus and, 147–48
  stress and, 40, 43, 44, 45
  taking care of, 64–65
physics, 129

Picasso, Pablo, 102
Pinterest, 35
play, importance of, 113–17,
    119–20
pleasure, experiencing, 35
politics, 97, 135
Pope, Alexander, 132
Porges, Stephen, 58
positivity, 8, 9, 10, 42, 48, 53, 71,
    90, 93, 115, 127, 134, 136
  bias, 127
  high-intensity, 71–73, 82
posttraumatic stress syndrome, 54,
    56–58, 61
practice, 96
prayer, 90
present, 11, 15–37
  benefits of living in the, 24–33
  bringing your mind into the,
    33–37
  charisma and, 30–33
  happiness and success in, 15–37
  overachievement and, 18–24
  practice consciously being, 33–34
  productivity and, 24–29
press, 1–2
Price, Evan, 35–36
productivity, 8, 9, 94, 155
  being present and, 24–29
psychological health, 8–9, 23, 40,
    136
  calm as key to energy manage-
    ment, 80–90
  cost of intensity, 70–80
  gratitude and, 136

  overachievement and, 23
  self-focus and, 147–48
  stress and, 40, 44, 45

regret, 29
rejection, 150
relationships, 9–10, 23–24, 134,
    141–64
  compassion for others, 141–64
  overachievement and, 23–24
  self-, 121–40
  self-focus and, 145–48
religion, 90
resilience, 11, 39–66, 130, 134,
    160
  breathing and, 55–63
  easing into your body, 64–65
  natural, 45–47, 54–59
  practicing, 61–65
  saboteurs, 47–51
  self-compassion and, 131–40
  stress and, 39–66
  tapping into 39–66
Rotman, Jackie, 16–17, 37
Ryan, Tim, 135–36

sadness, 8, 71
Scholes, Myron, 95–97, 109–10,
    113
Schooler, Jonathan, 100
self-compassion, 11, 12, 131–40
  gratitude and, 135–39
  making a habit of, 138–40
  phrase, 139
  power of, 131–40

self-confidence, 32

self-control, 70, 73–77, 84–85, 88, 92

  calm and, 84–85

self-criticism, 121–22, 125–29, 131, 134, 138, 140

  dangers of harsh, 125–29

  playing to your strengths and, 123–25

  self-compassion vs., 131–40

self-focus, backfiring of, 143–48

Seligman, Martin, *Authentic Happiness,* 20

serenity, 71

Severn, Sarah, 87

sex, 135

Shankar, Sri Sri Ravi, 55

silence, making time for, 110–13, 118–19

Silicon Valley, 15–18

Simmons, Russell, 88

sleep, 3, 10, 101, 136

  lack of, 70, 79

social media, 2, 3, 15, 21, 29, 108, 117

Sonnentag, Sabine, 93, 94

speaking skills, 32

Spencer, Herbert, 142

sports, 59, 65–66, 97, 120

Stanford University, 4, 15–18, 41, 43, 71, 95, 114, 130, 133, 150, 163

status, and compassion, 155–57

stillness, making time for, 110–13, 118–19

strengths, 123–25, 128–29, 136, 140

  believing in effort and, 129–31

  development of, 129, 130

  perils of playing to your, 123–25

stress, 2, 3, 5, 6–7, 18, 29, 40–45, 76, 81, 82, 88, 134, 136, 146, 150, 156, 160

  breathing and, 55–63

  hormones, 11, 59–60, 134, 163

  management failure, 51–54

  post-traumatic, 54, 56–58, 61

  resilience and, 39–66

  short-term vs. chronic, 43–45

  success and, 4–7, 39–45

  work, 23, 39–45, 146

subprime mortgage crisis (2008), 143

success, 2, 4–7, 39, 81, 122

  college and, 15–18

  compassion and, 148–61

  happiness and, 4–13

  myths of, 4–7

  in the present, 15–37

  self-compassion and, 131–40

  stress and, 39–45

Suess, Dr., 125

sugar, 51

suicide, 15, 83

suppressed emotions, 53

survival of the fittest, 142–43

swimming, 64

tai chi, 35, 65, 89

Taoism, 86

Tao Te Ching, 86
technology, 2, 15, 21, 25, 30, 35–36, 100
 taking a break from, 35–36
television, 41, 50, 53, 76, 88, 93, 105, 118
Tesla, Nikola, 98, 116
Thoreau, Henry David, 141
toughing it out, 51, 53
trustworthiness, and compassion, 155–57
Tsai, Jeanne, 41, 71, 72
Twenge, Jean, 144–45, 148
Twitter, 3, 15, 20, 21

vacations, 3, 42, 92, 97
veterans, 54, 56–58, 68
volunteerism, 161

walking, 64, 107, 118, 119
wandering mind, 28–29, 33, 34, 35, 99–120
 purposeful, 99–120
Watts, Alan, 15
Weber, Max, 30
Wegner, Daniel, 52, 77
Wieth, Marieke, 100
Wilde, Oscar, 73
willpower, 134
Wilson, Timothy, 105–6

Winfrey, Oprah, 88
work, 9–10, 18–19, 23, 142
 addiction, 18–24
 burnout, 68–69, 83
 compassion and, 141–47, 152–61
 creativity and, 98–99, 116, 118
 detaching from, 93–94
 gratitude and, 136
 happiness and, 9–10, 18–19
 love for, 91–92
 multitasking, 24–26
 perfectionism, 83
 performance evaluation, 128
 relationships, 145–47, 152–61
 self-control at, 73–77
 self-focus and, 145–47
 stress, 23, 39–45, 146
World War II, 81
worrying, 78–79
wuwei, 86

Yale University, 7, 121, 139
Yerkes-Dodson Law, 43–44
yoga, 35, 55, 64, 65, 89, 118, 119
 breathing exercises, 63
YouTube, 90

Zacks, Rose, 100

Greg Bledsoe

ABOUT THE AUTHOR

EMMA SEPPÄLÄ is science director of the Center for Compassion and Altruism Research and Education at Stanford University and co-director of the Yale College Emotional Intelligence Project at Yale University. Her field of expertise is health psychology, well-being, and resilience. This research was highlighted in the documentary film *Free the Mind*. She conducted groundbreaking research on mind–body practices for combat veterans and has also conducted research on meditation and compassion. Her research has been featured in the *New York Times, Forbes, The Boston Globe, U.S. News & World Report, The Huffington Post, Inc.,* and *Fast Company*. She has appeared on *Good Morning America, ABC News,* and *Fox News*.

She is founder of the popular online magazine *Fulfillment Daily* and has written for *Psychology Today, Harvard Business Review, The Huffing-*

ton Post, The Washington Post, Scientific American Mind, MindBodyGreen, and *Spirituality & Health.*

Seppälä consults for Fortune 500 leaders on building positive organizations. She regularly addresses academic, corporate, and governmental institutions.

She holds an undergraduate degree in comparative literature from Yale University, a master's degree in East Asian languages and cultures from Columbia University, and a Ph.D. in psychology from Stanford University.

Originally from Paris, France, she is a native speaker of French, English, and German.